OVERSTORY:
zero

For Sharon,
With much love,

—Bob—

OVERSTORY: zero

REAL LIFE IN TIMBER COUNTRY

Robert Leo Heilman

ROBERT LEO HEILMAN

Oregon Country Fair
Veneta, Oregon
1998

SASQUATCH BOOKS
SEATTLE

Printed in the United States of America.
Distributed in Canada by Raincoast Books Ltd.

Cover and interior design, cover and interior illustrations, and com-
position: Rohani Design, Edmonds WA

Library of Congress Cataloging in Publication Data
Heilman, Robert Leo, 1952–

    Overstory—zero : real life in timber country / Robert Leo
Heilman.

    p.cm.
    ISBN 1-57061-037-1 (hc)   ISBN 1-57061-084-3 (pbk)
    1. Heilman, Robert Leo, 1952– 2. Oregon—Biography.
3. Logging—Oregon. 4. Timber—Oregon. 5. Forests and
forestry—Oregon. I. Title.
CT275.H485A3 1995
979.5'043'092—dc20   95-12199

Sasquatch Books
1008 Western Avenue
Seattle, Washington 98104
(206)467-4300
books@sasquatchbooks.com
http://www.sasquatchbooks.com

Sasquatch Books publishes high-quality adult nonfiction and
children's books related to the Northwest (San Francisco to Alaska).
For information about our books, contact us at the above address, or
view our site on the World Wide Web.

"Remember, all of man's happiness is in the little valleys. Tiny little ones. Small enough to call from one side to the other."

— Jean Giono, *Blue Boy*

For Mrs. Stubkax,
without whom, nothing.

ACKNOWLEDGMENTS

The following essays appeared previously in other publications:
"Passes," "Eldorado," "The Smell of Home," "Honkers," "Falling
Ashes," "Central Heat," "Snow," "High Water," "Black Wings," and
"Upriver" in *The Umpqua Weekly Examiner*. "Central Heat," "Snow,"
"High Water," and "Eldorado" in "Northwest Public Affairs
Network." "An Occupational Disease" in *The Sun*, *The Oregonian's
Northwest Magazine*, *Forest World*, *KSOR Guide to the Arts*, and *The
Central Valley Times*. "Euclid's Hell" in *The Sun* and *Left Bank* #2. "Over-
story: Zero" in *Left Bank* #4, *Jefferson Monthly*, and *Northwest Passages:
A Literary Anthology of the Pacific Northwest from Coyote Tales to Roadside
Attractions*. "Diving High" in *The Oregonian's Northwest Magazine*.
"Getting By" in *Jefferson Monthly* (as "A Strange Recovery"), *The Ore-
gonian* (as "Quiet Mills, Slow Death"), and *The Congressional Record*
(as "Quiet Mills, Slow Death"). "Small Towns and Quiet Voices" in
Writers NW and *Jefferson Monthly*. "The Enemy Among Us or the
Enemy Within Us?" in *The News-Review* (as "Pain of Hard Timber
Choices Leads to Fear"). "The Field of Reality" in *Elysian Fields
Quarterly*. "Home of the Vigilantes for Justice," "Old-Timers," and
"Dirty Laundry" in *Jefferson Monthly*. "Fuji and the War on Young
Men" in *West Wind Review*. The excerpt on page v from *Blue Boy*, by
Jean Giono, is reprinted with permission of North Point Press, a
division of Farrar, Straus & Giroux, Inc.

"Although tree planting is part of something called reforestation, clear-cutting is never called deforestation—at least not by its practitioners. . . . On the work sheets used by foresters, a pair of numbers tracks the layers of canopy, the covering of branches and leaves that the living trees have spread out above the soil. The top layer is called the overstory, and beneath it is a second layer, the understory. An old-growth forest, for example, may have an overstory averaging 180 feet and an understory 75 feet. Clear-cuts are designated by the phrase 'Overstory: Zero.'"

⌐ from "Overstory: Zero"

CONTENTS

....

INTRODUCTION: THE QUESTION

$\mathbb{I}$ got stopped by a Douglas County sheriff's deputy last night for operating a motor vehicle that lacked a license plate light. I figured that he must be new around here. After all, I'd once driven my truck for two years with only a single headlight before I was finally told to fix it. The deputy was young, maybe a rookie, probably bored.

After he handed my papers back to me with a verbal warning, I mentioned, out of my bemused puzzlement, that I'd been driving that old pick-'em-up for twelve years and it had never had a license plate light in all that time.

"Well," he admitted sheepishly, "the reason we pull you over for that is to see if you're intoxicated, or driving without insurance, or on a wanted list somewhere."

"Gosh," I blurted out wistfully, "it's been a long time since I was any of those things."

It had been a decade or more since a local cop took even a passing interest in me, and I was flattered to find myself able to arouse suspicion on the night before my forty-third birthday. Ah, to be young and a suspicious-looking character again . . .

It's not easy to be seen as much of a threat after you've lived in the same small Oregon town for twenty years, even if you do look a little weird and drive a disreputable wreck. Maybe this book will change that.

I suspect it probably won't and certainly hope it doesn't. But there's always that risk when you present an intimate portrait of yourself and the people and the place you love to a national audience.

"What will the neighbors think?"

That's a question that in many ways defines what it is to live in a healthy, functioning community. Judging by the news from elsewhere, it's a question that fewer people than ever are asking themselves nowadays. It implies not only an obvious fear, but also the profound caring without which no community can long endure. It implies an adherence to local proprieties and a commitment to unmandated but essential duties. No one can force you to be a good neighbor, but to be considered one, you have to earn the distinction—no respect without being respectful and therefore respectable.

Respect is a difficult thing to learn and a harder thing to teach. As a baseball coach I found it to be the most worrisome part of the job—infinitely harder than losing two games out of every three, season after season. It's hard for kids to understand the connection between respect and winning ball games. As a man who has also umpired behind the plate, I can assure you that many adults don't seem to understand it either.

Nevertheless, I've had to "call 'em as I see 'em" too many times to do otherwise, whether on a ball field or in an essay. By and large, people respect that. They might not like it, but they respect it—and if people respect you long enough, they'll eventually forgive you for being wrong or (worse yet) right. They might even like you.

Tolerance is another aspect of real communities, ones that work because the people living in them have little choice but to make them work. There is hope too. When you live in a place where you rely on your neighbors and where you can readily see the good or ill effects of your own actions, it's easier to take responsibility for making your hometown a better place.

I feel very fortunate to live in such a community. It is a rare thing, and I've had a rare chance to examine it and to write about it. My hope is that some good will come from doing that, both for the small world that I and my neighbors inhabit and the larger world of which it is a small part.

I hope that by taking an honest look at our strengths and our weaknesses we can come to care more about our world and learn to respect it and ourselves and each other more. Then maybe—just maybe—if we care enough about each other and this place we call home, we can come up with some gifts that will have a lasting effect on our larger world.

~

Just as the world is made of many places and humanity is made of many individuals, so too, every place and every person has a multitude of aspects. All these aspects exist not in isolation but as pieces of an infinitely complicated whole.

Through these essays, memoirs, and sketches, I've tried to portray some of that complexity, to look at connections between my life and the lives of my neighbors, between our work and our place, our families and our community. It's not a bad place and not a bad life; both are flawed in many ways but blessed in just as many. It's impossible to separate my life from this place, or to analyze separately the uncountable aspects of either.

The aim of all autobiographical writing is apologetics, the saying, too late, of the things that should have been said. It is, of course, a foolish task, born of a desperate desire to be understood. Ultimately, it is a futile one as well, doomed from the outset by an innate dishonesty. Sometimes I think that the only honest writer was Lao-tzu, who had the good sense to admit defeat in the first line of the *Tao Te Ching*: "Existence is beyond the power of words to describe."

And yet, there is the hope that we may, at times, go beyond mere expression and actually say something useful.

⌒ Robert Leo Heilman
Myrtle Creek, Oregon

AN OCCUPATIONAL DISEASE

$\mathbb{I}$t was the damp, chill autumn time, barely too warm for frost and too wet for comfort. We were working on a Bureau of Land Management stream-cleaning contract, clearing out a logjam in the Siskiyou Mountains near the California line. My partner, Brian, and I sat up on the stream bank among sword fern and viny maple and waited to see what kind of fool the log would make of the government inspector.

The odds were about fifty/fifty that he'd shortly be a dead fool or a maimed one or even better, that he'd end up a cold wet one. Regardless, we sat in the fog-wet brush near the yarder's tailblock, me smoking a hand-rolled cigarette, Brian with a jab of chew in his cheek, not talking, keeping our thoughts under our hard hats.

Below us and about one hundred feet upstream, the inspector stood where I had stood an hour before, on a wet boulder, looking up at an old rotting log that hung overhead, wedged between moss-dappled rock walls above a small pool. Behind the log a waterfall fed the pool.

Standing there in midstream on the slick rock, with the sound of splashing water and the mass of the log above and before me, I'd seen the possibilities and didn't like any of them. If my chain saw didn't get stuck, if the log's compression didn't send it buckling my way, if I could shift my balance away from the log so that I didn't fall into the pool, if I didn't slip and fall, breaking an ankle or rib while scrambling out of the way, I would merely get drenched on a cold fall mountain morning.

From above, up on the bank, it had looked routine; but standing there on that rock I could see that it was lethal. I gave it up as too risky and then Brian walked down there, saw in hand, and came to the same conclusion. "It's funny," he said after climbing back up the bank, "it looks easy from here."

Now it was the government man's turn down there in the hole. He had showed up an hour later, looked down from the bank at the rock and log and pool, and declared the log removable. The contract specified a clear, debris-free channel and he was there to make sure we fulfilled the contract.

We refused. "It's not safe."

"Hell, I could cut it out of there myself."

"Okay—go for it," Brian said, and handed him a chain saw.

There was no use arguing with him. The log had fooled us too, until we stood in the only spot where you could lay a saw on it. If he wanted to prove us wrong, we'd give him the chance. The man might die, as easy as not. The log might crush him, pin him, or drown him. We would, of course, try our best to save his life afterward. But it was his choice now. Anything might happen—and to us it was all the same. Our hearts stayed as gray and featureless as a fog bank.

Though loggers are often portrayed as hard characters, neither of us was cruel or deliberately heartless. Our indifference to his fate could easily be ascribed to machismo, a matter of manful pride, or to class differences with the inspector, whose boast had challenged both our craftsmanship and our courage.

Logging is rough work. Hard labor, long hours, dangerous conditions, and male-only companionship almost guarantee a hardening of the heart. There's also the wear and the tear on your spirit from tearing up the world. Work gloves can protect soft hands, but tender psyches just develop calluses. Pride and the nature of logging go a long way toward explaining our attitude, but not far enough.

We are all loggers in our own way, though for most of us the brutality and violence of our jobs is more subtle. "I'm sorry," we say, "it's company policy," as if the rules of corporations were as real and immutable as the laws of nature. Alienation is an occupational disease, one that afflicts each of us when we sell our time for money. It brings a numbness of spirit that makes all sorts of horrible situations seem routine.

At work we become ashen-faced zombies, obediently carrying out tasks whose meaning and effects we seldom care about. We save real living for the weekends. Perhaps there is something in the nature of money itself that poisons all human relations it touches. Or maybe it's something in human nature that leads us to sell off our lives, to trade the possibility of love for a strictly limited security. Whatever the cause, ultimately it whittles us down to its own inhuman scale. Most people are likable enough away from the job and even at work. We each contain a complexity and beauty that art can never portray. We also contain a bleakness of spirit unimaginable. It is in the humdrum, the daily grind, the unreal world of work that we cross between the two without noticing the change.

One hundred feet away, down in the creek bed, the government man stood where Brian and I had each stood in turn. If he tried to cut that log, then he was a fool to doubt us and whatever happened to him was simply his own doing. We waited and watched as he started the chain saw and held it at arm's length overhead to start his cut. Wood chips cascaded down into the pool, exhaust smoke mingled with the morning mists. Then he stopped, withdrew the saw, shut it off, and came trudging back downstream and up the bank to where we sat.

"You're right," was all he said, and we were, of course, pleased to hear him admit it.

PASSES

In the eight hundred or so miles between San Diego and Redding, Interstate 5 climbs over one mountain pass, the Grapevine, between Los Angeles and Bakersfield. In the forty miles between Grants Pass and Canyonville, it takes a roller-coaster ride over four passes: Sexton Mountain, Stageroad Pass, Smith Hill, and Canyon Creek. Long-haul truckers who are new to the route mutter over their truck-stop coffee and curse the engineers who laid out the road. "When will it end?" they wonder, and "Couldn't they have found a better place to put a freeway?"

Sixty miles farther north and five hills later is the answer to the first question, and no, there's no other way it could have been squeezed through here. Welcome to Douglas County.

Call it ruggedness or just call it sheer orneriness, but the fact is that even the mountains and rivers here do things their own way, running east to west instead of north and south like everywhere else on the West Coast.

It's a tough place to pass through and an even tougher one to get around in. Neighbors living less than a mile apart but separated from each other by steep ridges often have to travel forty or fifty miles by road to visit. They might as well be on the backside of the moon.

We feel that we are more than just a little different from other Oregonians. Isolation breeds independence, a habit of mind that brings us some good-natured kidding from our neighbors to the north and south about being a backwater place, outside the mainstream of American life, a charge that rolls off the average Umpquan like rain off a mallard.

There's something to be said for living in a backwater. Considering the hodgepodge of fads, fashions, and politics that passes for American mass culture, being different can be a real blessing. We can go on quietly doing things our own way.

The mountains that cut us off also force us together, because isolation breeds interdependence as well as independence. Around here, being a good neighbor is much more important than your politics or your lifestyle or your religion.

Many folks who live here feel that we should seal off our mountain passes and secede from the state of Oregon and even the Union. But that's not really necessary. The mountains have already given us what we need: the twin gifts of orneriness and neighborliness. The secession has already taken place—in our hearts.

MONDAY MORNING

There's a yellow sheet of paper from a legal pad hanging on the office door next to the time clock. It lists, in red ink, the work schedule for the week. I find my name under the heading "Indefinite Layoff—Subject to Immediate Recall." Bob "Hielman," it says. The asshole didn't even spell my name right. What are the odds that he gave a thought to what that listing means for me and my wife and our baby? Winter, the recession, food stamps and government surplus cheese, Thanksgiving, Christmas, silent worrying nights of waiting for spring and an end to the housing slump. I thought I had it made.

The door that the work schedule hangs on, the wall that frames the door, the shelf that holds the time clock, the lockers behind my back are all the work of my hands. They are not art but they are well-crafted, functional pieces of industrial simplicity. They are the work of a journeyman carpenter and they look it. On Friday I looked at them with satisfaction. Now I just want to escape. I turn and walk out the door without saying a word.

The gas gauge on my 1962 Chevy Nova reads "E" and the starter solenoid won't catch in this cold weather. I sit clicking the key over and over again, listening to the starter whir without catching, and wonder if I'll end up walking the mile and a half home.

There's a tapping on my window. It's Tricia, and I roll down the window.

"What's up?" I ask.

"Hey, I've got an empty for you in the car," she says. "Wait a minute—I'll go get it."

I've got a one-cow dairy, and Tricia is one of my customers. I wait, watching the smoke from the wood-burner billowing out and up the side of the building. The stack stops about ten feet short of the roofline, and the smoke blackens the light green metal siding. It's a new building and ten feet of pipe could keep it looking new, but "pipe costs money," so the stain gets worse day by day, the paint blisters and peels; by spring it'll rust and the triangle of black soot will have a complementary red stain trailing downward. By spring I may have lost my place, and the cow with it.

Tricia comes back with a one-gallon glass jug. I take it from her and ask if she'll need another gallon on Wednesday.

"Yeah," she says. She's chewing gum and it makes her look like a tough broad. "Did ya see the notice?"

"Yeah."

"Bummer, huh?"

"Yeah, well . . . that's life, I guess." She's still working. Half the place is laid off and half is still employed. "It ain't the first time."

"No, I guess not," she says. "Jay and Fred are laid off too." And they also have kids to feed.

This time the starter catches on the first try. The asthmatic engine coughs up a little blood and I'm on my way.

This isn't the first time. It is merely another step in an unvarying pattern: hunt for work, find an employer who promises a decent living, work your ass off, get laid off and start all over again. All for substandard wages. Sometimes you get ripped off worse than other times, and once in a while you meet a decent boss you really like. But in southern Douglas County, Oregon, getting laid off is a fact of life.

I turn left at McCormick Piling's pole yard and start scanning the yard to see who's working and how much wood is on the skids. I see Calvin Poncho cutting knots off of a thirty-five-foot log with a double-bit ax; Carl Linde bent over a forty-footer, chipping away with his winter spud; and Leonard toting three peeled poles behind the jilly truck, backing up to the thirty-footer pile. Leonard is seventy-three and the other two are only ten years younger. Peeling the bark off of telephone pole logs is such brutal work that only old men can do it for long.

Young men are too lazy; the old men work because they must. They have worked hard all their lives and if they ever stop, they'll die. They chip away, steadily, patiently, every day, log after bark-clad log, leaving them clean and white for eight cents per linear foot. Calvin could use a chain saw to cut the knots, but none of them would ever do that. They prefer instead the bite of their keen axes.

There's quite a few loads of barkies in right now. If I go in later I might talk them into letting me have a load. They all know me from a summer that I spent working there as a yard man and I'm on fairly good terms with Norman, the farmer who manages the place. My upper back has been bad since the accident last fall, and the doctor says I'm supposed to avoid pole peeling, tree planting, roofing, and other stoop labor, but then, I'm not supposed to be doing carpentry either. If I take it easy, I can probably get away with it. We've got to eat, after all.

Across from the pole yard there's a big two-story house with twenty acres of prime bottomland. The house is well-kept and recently remodeled; the land is uncultivated briars and thistle. The place belongs to a likable middle-aged guy and his wife. He's a top-notch businessman but a piss-poor farmer.

....

Out in the front pasture is an Angus steer named Andy and a Shetland pony named Petunia. Andy's looking a little thin. He hasn't seen a bale of hay or a can of grain since I sold him to the businessman last August. At least the fall rains have brought up a little grass now, so he doesn't have it as bad as he did when the summer heat had the place all withered and brown.

The businessman owes me four hundred dollars for Andy. He was supposed to pay me on October 1, but his wife spent three thousand dollars on new furniture, so he's short on cash. I'll have to go see him today, because I don't have enough money to make my land payment this month. Knowing that it's a trivial sum for him makes it harder to ask for it. I don't want to think about how much I need that money.

The car bumps over the railroad tracks and I make the tight right turn that leads home. Weaver Road is a narrow gravel road that climbs steeply at first and then winds along the hillside above the tracks for three miles before dropping back down to cross the railway again and merge into the interstate. It is lined with oak and bigleaf maple that overreach the road in places, forming gold and brown tunnels of foliage.

It is a quiet road, used more by deer and squirrels than by cars. Sitting in my living room I can distinguish the arrival of my neighbors and the mail lady from the passing of strangers by the sounds of their engines. At night, high school kids roar past, sliding sideways

....

around the graveled corners, and the morning sometimes reveals a pair of panties hanging from roadside bushes. If I had a nickel for every midnight coupling, I wouldn't have to worry about the mortgage.

Diane is surprised to see me home so soon.

"No work today?"

I shake my head. "Laid off," I tell her, "indefinitely."

"Oh, shit!"

She has to go to school. I'll stay home and watch Kurt. We talk about the "dime-a-dip" fundraising dinner for Kurt-o's day-care center that we're going to tonight and kiss each other goodbye.

Mr. K is hungry. Usually he eats at the preschool but today he's home. I haven't eaten either, so we make breakfast together, him standing on a chair, bare-bottomed, making the toast, me at the stove, frying eggs sunny-side up and venison steak medium rare.

We sit down to eat at the oval oak table. The eggs are fresh from the hen house, the venison is from a tender spike buck who stepped in front of a friend's gunsights last week. The milk is this morning's, raw and whole, sweet with cream. In the country you can be broke and still eat better than a bank president.

O V E R S T O R Y : Z E R O

THE MAIN THING

The main thing is to have a big breakfast. It's not an easy thing to do at 4 A.M., but it is essential because lunch won't come for another seven or eight hours, and there are four or more hours of grueling work to do before you can sit down and open up your lunch box.

The kids on the crew, eighteen-year-olds fresh out of high school, sleep in an extra half hour and don't eat until the morning store stop on the way out to the unit. They wolf down a Perky Pie, a candy bar, and a can of soda in the crummy, good for a one-hour caffeine and sugar rush. They go through the brush like a gut-shot cat for a while and then drag ass for the rest of the morning.

But if you're a grizzled old-timer in your mid-twenties, you know how to pace yourself for the long haul.

You're exhausted, of course, and your calves, hips, arms, and lower back are stiff and sore. But you're used to that.

You're always tired and hurting. The only time you feel normal is when you're on the slopes, when the stiffness and fatigue are melted off by the work. It gets worse every morning until by Saturday it takes hours to feel comfortable on a day off. Sunday morning you wake up at four o'clock, wide awake and ready to stomp through downtown Tokyo, breathing fire and scattering tanks with your tail.

Your stomach is queasy but you force the good food into it anyway—a big stack of pancakes with peanut butter and syrup, four eggs, bacon, and a pint of coffee. There is a point when your belly refuses to take any more. Saliva floods your mouth and you force back the retching, put the forkful of food down on the plate, and light another cigarette.

It's dark outside and it's raining, of course. They aren't called the Cascades for nothing. It's December and the solstice sun won't rise until eight, three hours and a hundred miles from home, somewhere along a logging road upriver.

Raincoat and rain pants, hard hat, rubber work gloves, cotton liner gloves, and a stiff pair of caulk boots stuffed with newspaper crowd around the woodburner. All the gear is streaked with mud except the boots, which are caked with an inch-thick mud sole covering the steel nails. The liner gloves hang stiff and brown, the curving fingers frozen, like a dismembered manikin's hand making an elegant but meaningless gesture.

Mornings are slow. It's hard to move quickly when your stomach is bloated, your body is stiff, and, despite the coffee, your mind is still fatigue-foggy. You have to move though or miss your ride and lose your job. You try an experimental belch, which doesn't bring up too much half-chewed food with it and relieves the pressure.

The laxative effect of the coffee would send you to the toilet but your ride to town is due soon, so you save it for later. Better to shit on company time anyway, squatting out in the brush. It gives you a pleasant break, a few minutes of hard-to-come-by privacy, and it pisses off Jimboy, the foreman, since, being a college boy and therefore trained to worry about what people think of him, he could never bring himself to actually complain about it.

Lester the Rat taught him that lesson the first week of the season. Les had just planted a seedling and straightened up and turned his back on the slope to empty his bladder. The foreman glanced back to see him standing there with his back turned, staring idly across to the opposite slope.

"Hey, Gaines, get back to work! Let's go!"

The Rat turned to face him and shook the last golden drops off. He smiled pleasantly, showing a mouth full of crooked snoose-stained teeth. "Sure thing, Jim," he said mildly. "You bet." None of the professors up at the university had ever mentioned anything like that, and Jimboy blushed delicately while all up and down the line the crew snickered.

Jimboy makes more money than you do and doesn't work as hard, which is bad enough. But he's also afraid. It's his first winter on the slopes and he's not used to riding herd on a gang of brush apes. He also wants to make a good impression on his boss, the head forester, so he tries to push his crew into ever greater production. He sees himself as a leader of men, a rugged scientist overseeing the great work of industrial progress.

Everyone tries to get his goat so that, with any luck, he'll amuse us some day by breaking out in tears like Tommyboy, the last foreman, did. "You guys are just animals," Tommyboy had sobbed, setting off a delighted chorus of wolf howls and coyote yelps. It was the high point of the planting season and a considerable source of pride for the whole crew.

KAMIKAZES

There's a flash of headlights and the crunch of gravel in the driveway. Mighty Mouth awaits in his battered old Ford. You pull up your suspenders and start slapping your pockets: tobacco pouch and rolling papers, matches, bandanna, wad of toilet paper, pocket watch, jackknife, store-stop money—all there. You put on a baseball cap and a plaid woolen overshirt and gather up your gear: caulks, extra socks, rubber gloves, cotton liners, hard hat, rain gear, coffee thermos, and feed bucket. Then you step out into the rain.

There's nothing to talk about on the half-hour drive down the creek and downriver to the mill. You know each other too well by now, riding and working together twelve to fourteen hours a day—two moonlit rides and a picnic lunch every day—for three winters. The Mouth holds a beer bottle between his thighs and spits his chew as he drives.

You roll a cigarette and listen to the radio and peer out through the windshield, watching for the twin reflection of deer eyes ahead. The road is narrow and winding, the roadside brush thick, and you never know just when a deer will step out or leap, windshield-high, in front of you. Every day, somewhere on the drive, you see at least one fresh deer carcass on the road. Headlights dazzle the deer, and usually they stand frozen in their tracks before leaping aside at the last moment. Sometimes they leap toward the headlights though—always a suicidal move for the deer—but, like a kamikaze pilot, they can kill too.

CRUMMY TIME

The mercury-arc lamps light up the mill with a weird, hellish orange glow. Steam rises from the boilers and there's a sour rotting smell everywhere. The huge metal buildings bristle with an improbable-looking tangle of chains and belts and pipes. There's a constant whistling, clanging, and screaming of saws and machinery coming from them. Bug-eyed forklifts and log loaders crawl around the half-lit yards, mechanical insects scurrying to keep up.

Through the huge open doorways you can see the millhands at work in their T-shirts, sorting out an unending river of lumber and veneer into neat stacks. The mill workers sweat like desperate dwarves. They make more money than you and stay dry, but you feel pity and contempt for them. The poor bastards stand in one spot all night, moving to the computerized lightning rhythm of conveyors instead of their own human speed. The cavernous interiors of the mill sheds seem as cramped as closets compared to the open mountain slopes.

You work for the mill but not in the mill, on a company reforestation crew. Most of the company land is planted by contract crews, but the mill runs a crew that plants land the contractors won't touch—too steep or too ravaged, too old or too brushy.

Acres away, beyond the log pond, past the five-story-tall walls of stacked logs, next to the hangar-sized heavy equipment repair shop, is a small refrigerated trailer full of seedling trees in waxed boxes. Each box contains six hundred trees in bundles of fifty.

Mudflap and Sluggo are helping Jimboy load tree boxes into the back of a four-wheel-drive crew-cab pickup. They are young, straight out of high school, and eager to get a promised job in the mill come spring—if they "work hard and show up every day," of course. So they help load trees and ride with the foreman every morning.

You transfer your gear over to a mud-covered Chevy Suburban crummy. If you've ever ridden in one, you know why they're called crummies. The rig is a mess, both inside and outside. The seats are torn, the headliner is gone, the ceiling often drips from the condensed breath of its packed occupants. But you have a great fondness for the ugly thing. It is an oasis of comfort compared to the slopes.

We spend a large part of our lives roaring up and down river, powered by the Suburban's monster 454 V-8. Of course, none of this travel, or crummy time, as it's called, is paid time. Only the forty hours per week on the slopes earn us money. The other ten to twenty hours of crummy tedium are not the company's concern. Together with the half-hour lunch, also unpaid, we spend eleven to thirteen hours a day together for our eight hours' pay. All winter long we see each other more than we see our wives and children. We know each other intimately after so many cramped hours. We bicker and tease each other halfheartedly, like an old bitter couple, out of habit more than need.

ARITHMETIC

The ten of us plant about 7,000 seedling trees every day, or about 700 "'binos" apiece, enough to cover a little over an acre of logged-off mountainside each. It gets depressing when you start adding it up: planting 700 trees per day comes to 3,500 per week or 14,000 per month, which amounts to 56,000 trees in a season for one man planting one tree at a time.

Maybe you've seen the TV commercials put out by the company: helicopter panoramas of snow-capped mountains, silvery lakes and rivers, close-ups of cute critters frolicking, thirty-year-old stands of second growth all green and even as a manicured lawn, and a square-jawed handsome woodsman tenderly planting a seedling. The commercials make reforestation seem heartwarming, wholesome, and benevolent, like watching a Disney flick where a scroungy mutt plays the role of a wild coyote.

Get out a calculator and start figuring it: 700 trees in eight hours means 87.5 trees per hour, or 1.458 trees per minute—a tree punched in every 41 seconds. How much tenderness can a man give a small green seedling in 41 seconds?

Planting is done with an improbable-looking tool called a hoedag. Imagine a heavy metal plate fourteen inches long and four inches wide, maybe five pounds of steel, mounted on a single-bit ax handle. Two or three sideways hacking strokes scalp a foot-square patch of ground, three or four stabs with the tip and the blade is buried up to the haft. (Six blows 700 times amounts to 4,200 per day. At five pounds each, that comes to

21,000 pounds of lifting per diem, and many planters put in 900 to 1200 trees per day.)

You pump up and down on the handle, breaking up the soil, open the hole, dangle the roots down there, and pull the hoedag out. The dirt pulls the roots down to the bottom of the hole, maybe ten or twelve inches deep. You give it a little tug to pull the root collar even with the ground and tamp the soil around it with your foot. Generally, what's left of the topsoil isn't deep enough to sink a 'dag in, so you punch through whatever subsoil, rocks, or roots lie hidden by the veneer of dirt.

The next tree goes in eight feet away from the last one and eight feet from the tree planted by the next man in line. Two steps and you're there. It's a sort of rigorous dance, all day long—scalp, stab, stuff, stomp, and split; scalp, stab, stuff, stomp, and split—every 41 seconds or less, 700 or more times a day.

The ground itself is never really clear, even on the most carefully charred reforestation unit. Stumps, old logs, boulders, and brush have to be gone over or through or around with almost every slash-hampered step. Two watertight tree bags, about the size and shape of brown paper grocery bags, hang on your hips, rubbing them raw under the weight of the thirty to forty pounds of muddy seedlings stuffed inside.

Seven hundred trees eight feet apart comes to a line of seedlings 5,600 feet long—a mile and some change. Of course, the ground is never level. You march up and

....

down mountains all day—straight up and straight down. Although nature never made a straight line, forestry professors and their students are quite fond of them. So you climb a quarter-mile straight down and back up. Then you eat lunch and do it again.

It's best not to think about it all. The proper attitude is to consider yourself as eternally damned, with no yesterday or tomorrow—just the unavoidable present to endure. Besides, you tell yourself, it's not so bad once you get used to it.

O u t l a w s

Tree planting is done by outcasts and outlaws—winos and wetbacks, hillbillies and hippies for the most part. It is brutal, mind-numbing, underpaid stoop labor. Down there in Hades, Sisyphus thinks about the tree planters and thanks his lucky star every day because he has such a soft gig.

Being at the bottom of the Northwest social order and the top of the local ass-busting order gives you an exaggerated pride in what you do. You invade a small grocery store like a biker gang, taking the uneasy stares of lesser beings as your natural due. It's easy to mistake fear for a higher form of respect, and as a planter you might as well. In a once rugged society gone docile, you have inherited a vanishing tradition of ornery individualism. The ghosts of drunken bullwhackers, miners,

....

rowdy cowpunchers, and bomb-tossing Wobblies count on you to keep alive the 120-proof spirit of irreverence toward civilization that built the West.

A good foreman, one who rises from the crew by virtue of outworking everybody else, understands this and uses it like a Marine DI to build his crew and drive them to gladly work harder than necessary. A foreman who is uncomfortable with the underlying violence of his crew becomes their target. It is rare for a crew to actually beat up a foreman, but it has happened. There are many ways to get around a weak foreman, most of which involve either goldbricking or baiting. After all, why work hard for someone you don't respect and why bother to conceal your contempt?

B A G - U P

The long, smelly ride ends on a torn-up moonscape of gravel where last summer's logging ended. No one stirs. You look out the foggy windows of the crummy through a gray mist of Oregon dew at the unit. You wonder what shape it's in, how steep, how brushy, how rocky, whether it's red sticky clay or yellow doughy clay, freshly cut or decades old, a partial replanting or a first attempt. The answers lie hidden behind a curtain of rain, and you're not eager to find out.

The foreman steps out and with a few mutterings the crummies empty. Ten men jostle for their equipment in the back of the crummies. The hoedags and tree bags are in a jumbled pile. Most planters aren't particular about which bag they use, provided it doesn't leak muddy water down their legs all day, but each man has a favorite 'dag that is rightfully his. A greenhorn soon learns not to grab the wrong one when its owner comes around, cursing and threatening.

It's an odd but understandable relationship between a planter and his main tool. You develop a fondness for it over time. You get used to the feel of it, the weight and balance and grip of it in your hand. Some guys would rather hand over their wife.

The hoedag is a climbing tool, like a mountaineer's ice ax, on steeper ground. It clears the way through heavy brush like a machete. You can lean on it like a cane to help straighten your sore back, and it is the weapon of choice when self-defense (or a threat) is needed. It allows you to open up stumps and logs in search of the dark gold pitch, which will start a fire in a cold downpour, and to dig a quick fire trail if your break fire runs off up the hill.

The foreman hands out the big, waxed cardboard boxes full of seedling trees. The boxes are ripped open with a hoedag blade and the planters carry double handfuls of trees, wired up in bundles of fifty, over to the handiest puddle to wet down their roots. Dry roots will kill a tree before it can get into the ground, so the idea isn't purely a matter of adding extra weight to make the job harder—though that's the inevitable result.

Three to four hundred trees get stuffed into the double bags, depending on their size and the length of the morning's run. If the nursery hasn't washed the roots properly before bundling and packing, the mud, added water, and trees can make for a load that is literally staggering.

No one puts on their bags until the boxes are burned. It is an essential ritual, and depriving a crew of their morning fire is, by ancient custom, held to be justifiable grounds for mutiny by crummy lawyers everywhere. Some argue that homicide in such a case would be ruled self-defense, but so far no one has ever tested it.

The waxed cardboard burns wonderfully bright and warm. A column of flame fifteen feet high lights up the road, and everyone gathers around to take a little warmth and a lot of courage. Steam clouds rise from your rain gear as you rotate before the fire, like a planet drawing heat from its sun. It feels great and you need it, because once the flames turn to ashes you're going over the roadbank.

"Okay. Everybody get loaded and space out," the Mouth calls out. You strap on your bag, tilt your tin hat, and grab your 'dag. You shuffle over to the edge of the road and line up eight feet from the man on either side.

In the Hole

The redoubtable Mighty Mouth, the third-fastest planter, plants in the lead spot, and the men behind him work in order from the fourth- to the eighth-fastest man. It is a shameful thing to plant slower than the guy behind you. If he's impatient, or out to score some Brownie points with the boss, he'll jump your line and you plant in his position, sinking lower in the Bull-of-the-Woods standings. Slow planters get fired, and competition is demanded by the foreman.

There are many tricks to appearing to be faster than you really are—stashing trees, widening your spacing, pushing the man behind you into the rougher parts while you widen or narrow your line to stay in the gravy—but all of these will get you in trouble one way or another, if not with the boss, then worse still, with the crew.

The idea is to cover the ground with an eight-foot by eight-foot grid of trees. If mountains were graph paper this would be easy, but instead, each slope has its own peculiar contours and obstacles, which throw the line off. Each pass, if it follows a ragged line, will be more irregular than the last pass, harder to find and follow. It is difficult enough to coordinate a crew strung out over a hillside, each planter working at a different rate, going around obstacles such as stumps, boulders, cliffs, and heavy brush, without compounding it by leaving a ragged unmarked line behind for the next pass.

The two fastest planters, the tail men, float behind the crew, planting two to ten lines apiece, straightening out the tree line for the next pass. They tie a bit of blue plastic surveyor's tape to brush and sticks to mark the way for the lead man when he brings the crew back up from the bottom.

CUMULATIVE IMPACT

It's best not to look at the clear-cut itself. You stay busy with whatever is immediately in front of you because, like all industrial processes, there is beauty in the details and ugliness in the larger view. Oil film on a rain puddle has an iridescent sheen that is lovely in a way that the junkyard it's part of is not.

Forests are beautiful on every level, whether seen from a distance or standing beneath the trees or studying a small patch of ground. Clear-cuts contain many wonderful tiny things—jasper, agate, petrified wood, sun-bleached bits of wood, bone, and antler, wildflowers. But the sum of these finely wrought details adds up to a grim landscape, charred, eroded, and sterile.

Although tree planting is part of something called reforestation, clear-cutting is never called deforestation—at least not by its practitioners. The semantics of forestry don't allow that. The mountain slope is a "unit," the forest a "timber stand," logging is "harvest" and repeated logging "rotation."

On the work sheets used by foresters, a pair of numbers tracks the layers of canopy, the covering of branches and leaves that the living trees have spread out above the soil. The top layer is called the overstory, and beneath it is a second layer, the understory. An old-growth forest, for example, may have an overstory averaging 180 feet and an understory 75 feet. Clear-cuts are designated by the phrase "Overstory: Zero."

In the language (and therefore the thinking) of industrial silviculture, a clear-cut is a forest. The system does not recognize any depletion at all. The company is fond of talking about trees as a renewable resource, and the official line is that timber harvest, followed by reforestation, results in a net gain. "Old-growth forests are dying, unproductive forests—biological deserts full of diseased and decaying trees. By harvesting and replanting we turn them into vigorous, productive stands. We will never run out of trees," the company forester will tell you. But ask if he's willing to trade company-owned old-growth forestland for a reforestation unit of the same acreage and the answer is always, "No, of course not."

You listen and tell yourself that it's the company that treats the land shabbily. You see your frenzied work as a life-giving dance in the ashes of a plundered world. You think of the future and the green legacy you leave behind you. But you know that your work also makes the plunder seem rational and is, at its core, just another part of the destruction.

More than the physical exhaustion, this effort to not see the world around you tires you. It takes a lot of effort not to notice, not to care. You can go crazy from lack of sleep because you must dream in order to sort out everything you see and hear and feel during the day. But you can also get sick from not being truly awake, not seeing, feeling, and touching the real world.

When the world around you is painful and ugly, that pain and ugliness seeps into you, no matter how hard you try to keep it out. It builds up like a slowly accumulating poison. Sometimes the poison turns to venom and you strike out, at work or at home, as quick as any rattlesnake but without the honest rattler's humane fair warning.

So you bitch and bicker with the guys on the crew, argue with the foreman, and snap at your wife and kids. You do violent work in a world where the evidence of violence is all around you. You see it in the scorched earth and the muddy streams. You feel it when you step out from the living forest into the barren clear-cut. It rings in your ears with the clink of steel on rock. It jars your arm with every stab of your hoedag.

THE LONG MARCH

"War is hell," General William Tecumseh Sherman said, because, unlike a Pentagon spokeman, he was in the midst of it and could not conceive of something so abstract as "collateral damage."

"Planting sucks," we say, because unlike the mill owner who signs our paychecks, we slog through the mud and bend our backs on mountain slopes instead of reading progress reports on reforestation units. Like infantry, we know only weariness and hopelessness in the face of insanity.

"The millions of trees that the timber industry plants every year are enough to plant a strip four miles wide from here to New York," the foreman tells us.

Our hearts sink at the thought of that much clear-cutting, but Madman Phil, the poet, sees a vision. "Forward, men!" he cries. "Shoulder to shoulder we march on New York. The American Tree Planter! Ever onward!"

Someone starts it and then the whole crew is humming "The Battle Hymn of the Republic," while in our minds we cross the Cascades, the Snake River Valley, the Rockies, the Great Plains, and onward, ever onward, a teaming, faceless coolie army led by Walt Whitman, Sasquatch, and Mao Tse-Tung, a barbarian horde leaving a swath of green behind us "from sea to shining sea."

"Oh God!" Jimboy moans. "You guys are crazy."

During the Watergate summer of 1973, while Sam Ervin roasted Nixon administration witnesses, I worked as a roofer on a housing development in New Mexico. The days had an amazing sameness. The one-hundred-degree-plus weather held for weeks on end. Though there were six different floor plans for the housing units that we were building, they had only two roof styles—one with a skylight in front and one without. The shingles were either light or dark brown. Each roof took two days to lay. Every measurement, every vent, and each piece of metal flashing was the same as the roof before and the roof that followed. The gravel-coated asphalt shingles formed a Euclidean hell more arid and featureless than the surrounding desert.

Every day a certain cloud would form over the same peak of the San Juan range in the distance. When it grew to the right size, I would confirm with my pocket

....

watch what the cloud had already told me: lunchtime was at hand.

In the relative coolness beneath the roof we ate our meal with the assembled hard-timers, hippies, Chicanos, and Indians who made up the construction crews, and listened as the contractors argued. There were frequent arguments, sparked by trade chauvinism, conflicting schedules, and Methedrine.

One day the head electrician and the framing foreman got into it. The electrician drew out the blueprints for the house and pointed from the plans to the wall and back again, saying, "See? It calls for a doubled stud right here. How the hell can I hang a box here unless you double it up?"

The carpenter was nonplussed. "This place was screwed up from the get. The foundation's off, the slab's wrong. Face it: It wasn't built to the plan—it was built to the hill. You've got to make allowances."

Despite the fact that the carpenter really should have doubled up that stud, I remember feeling that there was something important about the exchange without really understanding its significance. Like a Sufi story, the carpenter's complaint came back to me over the years, always ringing true, but only slowly revealing its implications.

It was, I believe, the ancient conflict between what is and what ought to be, between the vision and the reality, between mind and matter, with mind stubbornly

....

insisting that its expectations be met and reality even more obstinately refusing to be something it isn't. "Wish in one hand and shit in the other—see which one fills up first," goes the proverb.

We were, as craftsmen, caught up in a no-win situation. Someone, or some group of somebodies, somewhere had created a plan, a vision set forth on paper, as clean and abstract as a problem in geometry. A housing tract, consisting of housing units, would rise on some lots. Every detail had been considered before-hand. It simply remained for us to follow the dictates of blue lines on white paper.

And yet, that paper village could never stand on this earth. Nature, both human nature and Mother Nature, ensured that.

Stubborn reality refused to conform to the unreal desires of mind. Each piece of the plan, when put into execution, asserted its own individuality against the mind that treated it as undifferentiated, interchangeable parts. No two houses could really be the same. No two nails, of the kegs we pounded, were identical; no two boards or shingles or grains of sand in the concrete were truly the same as any other that ever was or would be. A common everyday miracle prevented, once again, the drabness of human thought from reproducing itself. Walt Whitman would have been pleased.

It's amazing to me how little respect most people seem to have for reality. The mind is a wonderful thing and perhaps most wonderfully of all, it is capable of tricking us into accepting its version of what takes place around us. We repeatedly mistake our perceptions for the stuff of existence, even when we know better. Like a kitten trying to touch its image in a mirror, we reach out to the world we think we see, only to find that it's not really there.

I know many people who are terrified by the notion that reality is by nature incomprehensible. A very few are delighted by it. Most people, it seems, never take up the question at all.

I have heard and read about some of the reasons why so many of us trust our perceptions more than we trust the world as it is. It's difficult to sort them all out and get a clear picture, but it's not hard to see what happens when plans seem more real to us than what is actually there. Every act of mass destruction has a logical, and often noble, goal.

In the spring of 1980 I was finishing up my fifth winter as a tree planter in southern Oregon. It was my sixth crew in five seasons and by that spring I'd planted 150,000 seedling trees, enough to replant something close to three hundred acres of logged-off mountain slopes. At ten planters to a crew, I must have helped reforest about 3,000 acres, all within an eighty-mile radius of my home.

One morning we were planting some freshly clear-cut land up Buck Creek, a three-hundred-acre rocky, ravaged reforestation unit. Our crew was attempting to plant Douglas fir seedlings with ten-inch roots in a perfect eight-foot by eight-foot grid pattern in shallow, eroded soil and logging debris.

Over and over again, we bent our backs and swung our hoedags only to clink against rock covered with three or four inches of topsoil. We did what we could for the land, finding small pockets of soil built up on the backside of the huge, sap-oozing stumps of the forest that used to be and scratching holes in the shallow spots as proof that we'd been there and found the spot unplantable.

"Shit!" someone spat after yet another arm-jarring clink. "I feel like a goddamn chicken scratchin' around out here."

"Buck-buck-buh-gawk! Buck-buck-buck-buck-buh-gawk!" I answered, and the rest of the crew took up the call.

It was spring, a beautiful, sweet-smelling sunny day, and a sort of madness overcame us, compounded of ten wiry bodies in motion, sunshine, and the frustration of the work. We glanced over our shoulders slyly, challenging Jack, the foreman, to stop our clucking insurrection.

Jack surveyed the scene from his stump-top roost, leaning against his inspector's shovel. He lifted his hard

....

hat, scratched his head, and decided to try to change the subject. As was his wont, he spoke of the wonders of modern forestry.

"Boy, they sure did a nice job on this unit. Lots of reprod." He gestured toward some scraggly residual trees. "The loggers sure pissed and moaned when we made 'em get good suspension, but those naturals will really take off now that we let the sunlight in. In the old days we wouldn't have bothered, you know. Hell, ten years from now this'll all be thick as dog hair with young firs."

"Fuck-fuck-fuck-fuck-off!" someone down the line called out amid the clucking and chinking. Jack pretended he hadn't heard.

I thought of the hardscrabble canyons of Rock Creek, of the old units logged twenty and thirty years ago that we'd replanted all winter long, trying for the fifth or sixth time to bring back the forest on land whose soil had been muddying the river for decades. Something sad and ugly rose within me. I stood up, leaning on my hoedag to straighten my sore back, hitched up my tree bags to ease the chafing on my hips, and turned to face my foreman.

"You're nuts," I told him. "This is totally fucking insane." I gestured downstream at the silted creek bed, at the place where we'd found chips of jasper knapped from tool cores by the Indians, at the stark gray face of Buck Rock gleaming in the sunlight for the first time in

....

ten thousand years, at the yarder tower roaring its diesel roar and hooting like an owl as it dragged a turn of logs uphill to the waiting log trucks.

"Look at this place, Jack. This ain't a forest—it's a disaster. Get your head out of your ass and look at it. A hundred years from now people will wonder how the hell we could have been so fucking stupid."

The clucking had stopped. The rest of the crew stood still, grinning and watching and waiting to hear Jack's reply.

"This is good ground. This unit will come back just fine. We've done a good job logging it, the best anybody can do, with all the best techniques we've got, and it'll come back just fine."

It was time to back off. I knew that. It was one thing to bait the man as a joke, but challenging his profession was stepping over the line. I couldn't back off, though. The accumulated poison of five winters of tree planting had turned to venom.

"Bullshit. You're fucking crazy. All you company foresters are insane. Just look at this place, Jack. Take a look around you and see what's really going on here. It's totally insane."

"Look, Heilman, don't fuck with me. I run a good crew and we do good work. What do *you* know anyway? Huh? I've got a master's degree in forestry—I know what I'm talking about. You don't know shit," he said, as if mountains were blackboards.

I'd blown my next winter's job, his tone said. I thought of November and the uncertainty of finding another crew to work on. In the ten years since dropping out of high school I'd been laid off, fired from, or quit thirty different jobs.

"Yeah, what do I know? I'm just a dumb-ass tree planter."

"Shut up and get back to work."

I glanced at the last seedling I'd planted, chose a likely spot eight feet away for the next one, took two steps, and swung my hoedag. Up and down the line the laughter and clucking had died, and the only sounds were the scraping and clinking of hoedags on rocks and the distant roar of the yarder.

Jack wasn't a bad guy to work for at all. In fact, I liked him and respected him a good deal. It's not easy to ride herd on a bunch of mud-spattered brush apes and he did it well. But like a lot of nice people, he'd bought into a plan, some words on paper that he never questioned despite the evidence all around him. In his view, the plan itself was foolproof. If anything went wrong, it had to be because the plan hadn't been executed properly. It never occurred to him that no plan, no matter how detailed, could ever encompass something as complex and miraculous as a mountain slope.

The lack of respect for individuality makes all sorts of horrors and cruelties not only possible but seemingly desirable. After all, if the universe is composed of inter-changeable pieces, the annihilation or impoverishment or demeaning of any one piece, whether a rock or a mountain, a tree or a forest, a person or a people, a valley or a planet, cannot have much importance.

The underlying integrity of the cosmos is its infinite individuality. You can call it the thumbprint of the Creator, or simply mutter along with the carpenter that "You've got to make allowances," but the important thing is to honor it.

The illusion of sameness creates a devalued cur-rency in our language, thoughts, and emotions. We forget that the word only stands for the thing suggested, and the object itself is, by its essential nature, unknow-able mystery and sacred—simply by being.

Uniformity is a convenient fiction, useful for fool-ing ourselves but useless for seeing things as they really are. Never trust anyone who believes in the reality of units. They have sold their share in living for counter-feit coinage.

ELDORADO

His talk is both too proud and too modest and there's always the suggestion that he knows more than he says, though of course, he'll never come out and admit it. There's never any talk about what he's doing right now, or where, or exactly how or how much. But he's onto something that might or might not be happening or is about to happen, and make no mistake about that. Because it's there all right, just like the old-timers always said it was—everybody knows that.

It's profoundly rude to inquire too closely or to show any sign of doubt. All gold miners are honest and all are close-mouthed about their present circumstances. No, it's best to talk about the past and hear the tales of lost lodes and sudden finds, of years of diligent search abandoned just a few short feet away from staggering hidden wealth. It's best just to listen.

Eldorado, the golden one, surely lives on here. You can hear the echo of his footsteps in the mountain canyons—just around the bend. It sounds like a shovel digging through gravel, like wet sand sloshing back and forth in a metal pan. You can see his gleaming dust and flakes and nuggets, like pieces of the sun fallen to earth as a gentle rain.

It's nobody's business just how many ounces of the stuff come out of these hills every year—not yours or mine or the tax man's. It comes from no one says where and stays somewhere with someone or goes somewhere else, unmentioned except as a vague passing hint that there's more, always more, where it came from.

No one can say just how much it's really worth. But whatever it comes to in dollars, it's small pickings compared to the fever that grips our imagination. We can live without the gold but not without the pursuit of it, and a mine that stays lost is worth more than one found. All the wealth that might be scraped out from the dark underworld to gleam in the sunlight and delight the eye is still less precious than the golden dream itself.

GETTING BY

"While the 1979–1985 years were disappointing for wood products manufacturers and workers alike, the net result may well have been a blessing in disguise for the survival and long-term health of the industry. Hundreds of inefficient sawmill, veneer and plywood plants have been shut down. Others have been modernized and streamlined to achieve maximum return per unit of product. New products have been developed which require lower labor costs, cheaper raw materials, and result in a better value to end-user. The net effect is a leaner, more productive and cost-effective industry.

"One of the principal means of reducing costs, of course, is to lower wage rates."

⌐ Development Report and Plan,
CCD Business Development Corp.
Roseburg, Oregon, July 1986

I used to work for a white-haired old gyppo logger who taught me many things about living and working around here. I remember one morning when he told me about the recession of 1958. We were taking a coffee break in the little two-man sawmill he'd built with discarded equipment and old truck parts. As he talked, we watched a sparrow building her nest in the rafters of the mill shed.

It was 1978, and timber industry wages and per capita income levels in Douglas County, Oregon, where I live, were at an all-time high.

"They used to call them panics," he said, "and then it was depressions, and nowadays they call them recessions, but it's all the same thing. Every time things get rolling good, to where there's lots of small outfits working, money gets tight and the bottom falls out of everything. Then, after the smoke clears, you look around and most all the little guys are gone and the big outfits are bigger than ever."

That particular slump, back in 1958, had cost him his home and his sawmill. He went to work in northern California as head sawyer of someone else's mill. He stayed a few years, long enough to gather up a grubstake and return home to begin again. "A man does what he has to do to get by," he said.

In 1982, during Ronald Reagan's experiment in supply-side economics, the "trickle-down" recession, unemployment in Douglas County rose to 17.2 percent and per capita income dropped to 77.4 percent of the national level.

No 1982 figures are available for the rate or amount of emergency food usage because almost no emergency food was distributed in Douglas County. About 93,000 people lived here then, as now, and they probably would have eaten nearly a million pounds of emergency food that year, as they have every year for the past seven years. But there was no emergency food, only the need.

Even if available, numbers wouldn't tell the truth— not enough of it anyway. Besides, I don't trust numbers. People care about what they can understand in their hearts, and only machines, or perhaps machine-souled people, can take numbers into their hearts.

The tragedies of humanity are everyday tragedies. They can't be expressed as percentages or as issues. They are real and personal sufferings and deserve to be spoken of in a way that numbers and jargon can't communicate; that is to say, one should tell the truth, something numbers and jargon never convey.

In the spring of 1981 I sat sharing a forty-nine-cent quart of beer with a friend of mine. It was about eleven o'clock in the morning in the middle of the week, but neither of us had anything better to do. We were both out of work. He'd been laid off and I'd been disabled by a fall from a house roof.

From the front porch of his rented mobile home we could see across the trailer court to the creek where the willows wore their new greenery. His daughter and my son, both preschoolers, played on the lawn. The buzzards had returned to the valley, making the arrival of the new season official, and we drank and talked about the economic slump and the prospects of finding work for the summer.

"My dad told me the other night that there's a plan for this area," he said as we passed the bottle back and forth. His father was an accountant and a local business consultant. "He says the mills are going to stay shut until everyone who can afford to move leaves. The mills are all automating and whoever's left will be the people who can't go anywhere else and they'll work cheap. It's going to be like Arkansas or Mississippi around here—no more good wages."

"It wouldn't surprise me," I said, just to be agreeable, although I honestly thought I was hearing yet another conspiracy theory. Something in my tone of voice must have betrayed my doubt.

"No, really," he insisted. "I don't mean to say that this recession's all been rigged. They're just going to take advantage of it is all. The owners are all going to use it to get people to work cheap. Once everybody gets hungry enough, we'll all take pay cuts just to go back to work. They're talking about 'cost-effectiveness' and 'competitive wages' and like that."

There was an inescapable logic to what he was saying, almost like an algebraic equation: Hungry people work cheap; people who work cheap go hungry.

"Well," I said, "you're probably right. I don't know. Nothing we can do about it anyway. We'll just have to wait and see how it all turns out."

That summer I bought a Brown Swiss milk cow named Marygold and raised a flock of Rhode Island Red laying hens. Every day Mary gave about four gallons of milk, and the hens laid about a dozen eggs. I began selling the milk and eggs to my friends at cost, charging enough to cover the feed but not my labor. I found a baker who wanted raw milk and fresh eggs for his family and began bartering a dozen eggs for a loaf of bread or two loaves for a gallon of milk. I had a dozen families on my route, all friends of mine, all young, all married couples with children.

I let them have the food on credit and allowed them to pay in barter (poached venison a few times) or in food stamps when they didn't have the cash. Somehow there was always enough cash for a bale of alfalfa hay or a sack of grain when I needed it.

All this was illegal, of course, but laws aren't something you consider when you're hungry. Poor people break laws as a matter of survival; corporations break laws as a matter of business acumen. Like most of my neighbors (and all of my friends), I lived as the pettiest sort of criminal—driving without car insurance, selling raw uninspected milk and not reporting the income, accepting food stamps without authorization, cutting firewood without a permit, eating poached salmon and venison.

It's not something I'm proud of, nor particularly ashamed of either. Pride and shame were luxuries we couldn't afford at the time. Many times the jug of milk and carton of eggs that I dropped off were all a family had to eat. We were friends. We had children. We did what we had to do to get by. Even so, most of us didn't survive with our families intact.

When the unemployment insurance checks ran out, our little towns started to empty. "For Rent" signs appeared in house windows on every street. Families sold everything that wouldn't fit in the back of their pickup trucks to raise money for the trip to wherever the rumors said there was work.

Dan and Joy held their moving sale just before Christmas and left for Texas with their three sons right after the New Year. Dan had been down to Houston to scout it out and was happy to be doing something—anything—for a change.

"It's not like around here," he told us. "There's all kinds of work, not just the woods or the mill. The pay's not as good but there's steady jobs and all kinds of stuff for the kids to do, concerts and parks and stuff."

It was their last day in the valley and all of their friends were over. They stood among their packed possessions, giving away houseplants and knickknacks that hadn't sold. I pulled my pickup alongside the house and we loaded up the remainder of the firewood.

"That goddamn Bob," Dan laughed. "Instead of going out and cutting him a load, he just waits and burns your wood after you're gone."

We all laughed because it was true.

"That's okay," he added, "I won't need no fuckin' firewood in Texas."

They left the valley the next morning and by the following Christmas they were divorced. Dan was managing a fast-food place in Dallas, and Joy was living on the streets of downtown Houston and sleeping in an all-night movie theater.

Despite the larger horrors there was also much beauty in the little things we did—uncountable acts of kindness and love that made the times more bearable, but in the end weren't enough to keep us going on.

Bit by bit we lost our self-respect as we knocked up against hard realities and even harder institutions and agencies that were indifferent to our humanity. It was a slow process, one that we feared but couldn't really see happening.

It's hard to wait when you're used to working. There's a slow, steady erosion that wears down a few people first, and then whole families crumble like dirt clods running through your fingers. Finally the community itself is gone, washed downriver, never to return.

One by one the families broke up—nine out of twelve couples divorced within six years. Three of my friends, all men, died violently.

Numbers again, cold and flat, devoid of sorrow or joy, of dignity or beauty. Where is the formula that can calculate the supply and demand of affection? We can easily show that x amount of dollars spent on wages lowers profitability by n%, but where is the algebra to calculate human suffering?

I'd like to think that the survival of myself, my wife, and my son was due to right living and perseverance on our part, that somehow we got by when others didn't because of our individual and familial strengths. It would be a comforting notion if I only could believe it. But I'm convinced that it was simply the result of a statistical fluke.

At haying time, in the early summer of 1984, I attended a presentation put on by The Hunger Project. The physical therapist who was helping me out talked me into going. He felt that hunger was an important issue.

The affair was held at a church and began with brief statements by each of us on who we were, what we did to earn our daily bread, and why we were interested in hunger. I thought about introducing myself as a bank president or a wild-animal trainer but ended up telling the truth, that I was an unemployed laborer and that my great-grandmother had starved to death in southern Russia during the 1920s. One other guy introduced himself as an unemployed laborer, but no else mentioned any relatives who'd died of hunger.

We saw a slide show and listened to a presentation about infant mortality rates in central Africa and Iceland and sanitary conditions in Asia and Latin America. We were told about the global military budget and the amount that Americans spend on dog food and that the end of hunger as a global issue was an idea whose time had come.

There was a lunch break after the slide show, and everyone sat outside in the golden noon eating fruit and nuts and drinking juice. I walked across the street to a corner market and bought a beer and a bag of pretzels. When I returned I sat down across from the man who'd introduced himself as an unemployed laborer.

He didn't look like a working man and I was curious about him. I asked him what manner of work he was used to doing and learned that he had actually been an assistant something-or-other for a large corporation in a major city. He'd quit his job to become involved with social issues and moved his family to Douglas County, attracted, apparently, by the large number of poor people here. He was making a little money as a handyman and looking for blue-collar employment.

"We've adopted a lifestyle of voluntary poverty," he told me.

"You're kidding!" I gasped. It was as if he'd told me he had chosen voluntary toothache. I was stunned.

I knew, of course, that there was such a thing. The nuns who'd taught me as a child practiced personal poverty in favor of a modest communal wealth, and they told us countless stories about saints who'd given up silks and palaces for hair shirts and caves. But they at least expected a spiritual reward, not insight into an issue or empathy with the oppressed.

I had also read about the Russian intellectuals of the late nineteenth century who adopted peasant dress and built picturesque little villages to live "the simple life." But all of their empathy hadn't kept the famines away, and later, when Stalin's Five-Year Plan brought slavery and death to so many of my relatives, those same intellectuals provided the rationale for genocide.

Sitting there at a picnic table in a sunny churchyard among smiling Unitarians, I realized that I was in a very dangerous crowd.

By the fall of 1985, there weren't enough of my friends still living in the valley to cover the cost of feeding my cow. I sold her and her calf at auction and waited for the trickle-down.

It was a long time coming, that trickle-down. Ten years later we're still waiting for it. The mills and businesses and government agencies recovered, but the recovery never arrived for the people who live here. For the first time in our county's boom-or-bust economic history, business boomed while people stayed busted.

Davey was my neighbor's son when we lived in town. He and I worked on the same tree planting crew for a local mill during the winter of 1976. In the spring of that year he got a job in the mill. He was eighteen, fresh out of high school and earning $5.35 an hour.

In the spring of 1986 I ran into him in the grocery store. He'd been out of work for nearly a year but had just landed a job in another mill. He was grateful to have found work, which I could understand since he was now twenty-eight, married, and a father.

"Well, that's good to hear." I congratulated him. "How much are you making?"

"$4.75 an hour."

I should have kept my mouth shut. But a little mental arithmetic told me that, given the inflation rate, he was earning about half the pay he had as a raw kid.

"Jeeze! You guys are still eligible for food stamps," I blurted.

He looked away, over at the stacked boxes of margarine, before he spoke.

"Yeah, well, actually I'm getting more than most of the guys because I've got experience. Starting pay's $4.00 an hour."

It was an odd sort of recovery. Employment rates, timber harvest levels, and emergency food use rose. The cost of cutting, hauling, and milling a million board feet of timber dropped and so did wages and per capita income. Timber harvest levels for Douglas County were 400 million board feet higher in 1986 than in 1978 but produced $55 million less in wages. While the timber industry has become "leaner, more productive and cost-effective," the people have simply become leaner.

In 1989 the seventh straight year of economic recovery brought one in six Umpquans in for emergency food boxes or soup kitchen meals. Local relief agencies estimate that less than 5,000 pounds of emergency food were distributed annually in Douglas County in 1976–79. From 1986 through 1989 the 94,000 people living on the Umpqua ate nearly a million pounds of emergency food every year. None of us foresaw that back in 1976 when Davey and I were planting trees, except perhaps our foreman, Dan.

One morning, toward the end of the season, we drove to work through a bright silvery fog. We loaded up our tree bags in an eerie setting of impenetrable light. The crewmen were a little uneasy and someone cracked a joke:

"Hey boys, I think we're in big trouble—I thought I saw Rod Serling standing by the gate when we came through."

"All right, men," Dan announced after the laughter died down, "this is it. It's 1976 and the end of the world is here. The Lord's coming for us today, so I want you all out there planting good trees when our time comes." We laughed a little uneasily, strapped on our tree bags, shouldered our hoedags, and trudged off into the shining haze.

THE POLITICS AND PREJUDICE

OF OLD GROWTH

"There are many fine things that we cannot say if we
have to shout."

⌐ Henry David Thoreau, *Walden*

Fear has a way of sneaking
up on you. It's an odd, unsettling moment when you
realize that you've been afraid for a long time and have
been trying to hide it from yourself.

For me, the moment came on a sunny August
morning in 1988 when I stood on Main Street in
Canyonville, Oregon, a small town near my home. I had
brought my son and his friend to the annual Pioneer
Days parade. The boys were having fun, dashing out into
the road to scoop up candy tossed from the passing floats
and old cars. My niece marched by, decked out in calico
and a sun bonnet. My nephew strode past, banging the

bass drum in the Days Creek Marching Band. I always feel comfortable and expansive at small-town parades, like Walt Whitman in the crowd or everybody's kindly uncle, soaking up the joyful sounds, the gaudy colors, and the cheerful faces of my family and neighbors.

The parade had something new that year though. One of the floats was draped in yellow ribbons and featured a logger in hickory shirt, red suspenders, and hard hat wielding a chain saw. He mimed the act of falling a fir tree with a tree-sitting hippie doll tied to the top. The tree leaned precariously toward the truck bed, which carried a banner asking, "Who Will Hit the Earth First?"

My heart sank as my neighbors laughed. I realized that the doll was a caricature of myself and many of my friends, long-haired and bearded. I imagined the horror of actually being up in one of those groaning giants in flight. Having worked as a timber faller, I knew the tension that comes when cutting down one of the big old trees. I heard again the cracking of wood during the back cut, the creaking and whooshing of the tree in flight, and the apocalyptic roar made by tons of wood striking the ground.

Of course, I understood it all. It would be difficult to find a Northwest county more dependent on the timber industry than ours was. I knew that my neighbors were frightened, running scared in the face of an uncertain future. But now I found that anyone who even looked like they might disagree with the local majority was bearing the blame. Simply by my appearance, I had become an outsider in my own community.

It occurred to me later that these timber workers and their families were wonderfully good-hearted people who'd been inexplicably maligned. I realized that the float was not really an expression of hatred so much as a derisive reaction to a public debate in which the proud title of "logger" had become a pejorative term. It was a sort of perverse acceptance, through parody, of the role they'd found themselves saddled with: heinous men with chain saws. Our slander always says more about us than about our enemies, and all too often it shapes their character to fit our fears.

Of course, I don't fear my neighbors, the people I know and who know me. To know, to really *know*, someone is an act of love, requiring patience and an open mind. But what about those who only think they know me, who have fixed notions about categories of people— notions that keep them from seeing individuals?

It's much easier to hate (or love) a class of people than a particular person. People are complex. There's always something about an individual that gets in the way of our prejudice. "Am I not vast enough to contain contradiction?" asked Walt Whitman. Aren't we all?

I, too, yearn sometimes for pat answers and the reassurance of dogma. I almost wish sometimes that I could be a bigot. It takes me a lot of work to really know people. I have to listen to them and watch them and learn about their past, their hopes and fears, their lives. It's terribly time-consuming. It is also heart-rending.

Much of the frustration that environmental and industrial activists feel stems from the failure of confrontational politics to resolve the forest management dispute. Traditional political debate is limited in what it can address, working well with specific issues that can be decided with a simple vote. Unfortunately, the system, with its short-term piecemeal approach, isn't able to resolve complex long-term, fundamental problems. The social, economic, and environmental crisis brought on by forest management is at heart a cultural and scientific problem, not a political one.

A debate between government agencies, political organizations, and corporations is bound to lack a human dimension. Institutions simply don't have hearts, and by nature they discourage compassion.

In the spring of 1986, two years before that memorable parade, I helped organize and run a bioregional conference in Ashland, Oregon. Four hundred political activists gathered to take a "holistic approach" to dealing with social, economic, and environmental problems in southern Oregon and northern California. For well over a hundred years the people in this region have called it the "State of Jefferson," in recognition of its uniqueness. But for the occasion it had been dubbed "The Klamath-Siskiyou Bioregion," which had an aura of sociological legitimacy that the traditional name lacked.

Although there was a great deal of talk about seeing our region as a whole, crossing class lines, and working democratically for the benefit of everyone, it became obvious that "we the people" really meant "we the people who think alike" rather than "we the people who live here."

A workshop on "Long-Term Environmental Activism" turned out to be a group of environmentalists talking about the dangers of learning to like some of the government and timber industry officials they were forced into contact with. It was agreed that familiarity with their opponents carried a terrible risk of being "co-opted" into accepting a compromise. For an hour these earnest, well-intentioned activists searched for ways to maintain purity of purpose in the face of friendliness without ever mentioning compassion.

Failing to take the true measure of opponents is an all-too-common failing among political activists. It has brought sudden disaster to many movements and opened the way for unintended harm despite the best intentions and most noble aims. The problem is that no matter how exact the measurement, the end result is only an approximation.

Faced with inevitable imperfection and the impossibility of actual uniformity, craftsmen speak of tolerances. If a measurement falls within a certain range it's "close enough," because no matter how similar two of a kind may be, in the end there's really only one of each.

But somehow, although we know this on the physical level, we don't seem to understand that this is true of people too: no two people are exactly alike. People often insist on a lack of tolerance in dealing with each other.

We use words to measure people. But words, particularly in political discussions, are very unreliable measuring tools. Unless we constantly test them against what we actually see occurring, we run the risk of fooling ourselves with notions that have an internal logic that doesn't match up with reality.

Words are not only the tools of my trade but the raw material as well. I love the language, yet I distrust it—as any artisan must who respects both the work and the material. I've spent too much time practicing artifice to put much faith in words.

I once saw a magician sitting at a table alone between performances, playing solitaire with a deck of cards. I felt an immediate kinship with him because my own years of practicing the techniques of persuasion have left me as lonely as he was. In his case, it was society's distrust of his dexterity that left him unable to join a card game; in my case, it is my skill at sleight of mind that leaves me unable to trust the players in any political game.

The stereotypes of "preservationists" and "timber barons" have just enough truth in them to reinforce the images. Some mill owners really are greedy, some mill workers and loggers are truly ignorant and brutal, some environmentalists are in fact utterly insensitive to the needs and outlooks of blue-collar workers. But these individuals are actually rare. The few truly narrow-minded ones I've met are simply pathetic people whose dismal lives lead them to seek self-worth through political activism. Industrial and environmental extremists are actually much more similar to each other than they are to the moderates within their own camps.

Chuang-tsu, the Taoist philosopher, wrote, "When wrestlers pit their strength against each other, they begin in a lighthearted, open frame of mind but they usually end up looking angry. At the height of the contest, many crafty tricks are played." When push comes to shove, the further apart two sides grow, the more they become the same.

During the winter of 1979–80 I worked on a tree planting crew. I became friends with Steve Hoeffler, a planter from Monterey, California, who had been working for the Forest Service here in Oregon for a few summers and planting trees during the winter.

One day at lunch, Steve told me about his younger brother, who lived in Santa Cruz, California. His brother, inspired by Edward Abbey's *The Monkeywrench Gang*, had been vandalizing logging equipment on the weekends.

I thought about Stewart Clason, an old gyppo logger who'd taught me timber falling and logging. I imagined him coming to work in the morning to find his geriatric equipment vandalized.

"Jeezus, what a jerk," I said.

"Yeah, I told him to cut that shit out. It's stupid," he sighed, "but he thinks he's some kind of warrior or something. I tried to tell him that if he really wants to change things, he ought to get a job setting chokers and get to know the guy and then talk to him instead of sneaking around and messing up his show. The dumb shit's never worn a pair of caulk boots in his life."

Three years later, Steve ran a garden hose from his pickup's exhaust pipe into the cab, leaving a bright-red corpse for the sheriff's department to investigate. He was working for the U.S. Forest Service at the time, in the timber sales department at Tokettee Ranger Station on the Umpqua National Forest. I went upriver to visit him about a week before he killed himself. He'd broken up with his girlfriend three weeks before and was camping out in the woods by himself.

He didn't talk about the breakup much. He talked mostly about his gloomy outlook on the environmental health of the planet in general and the over-cutting of old growth in Umpqua National Forest in particular, and of how tired he was getting of being put down at work by the rest of his timber sales crew for being "that goddamn environmentalist." He told me that he'd been very lonely, living like that.

Based on ignorance, born in fear, driven by tension and frustration, and nurtured by demagoguery, prejudice follows a five-step path of escalating action. The first step is slander, which gives it a voice. Then comes avoidance of the hated group, making the lies easier to believe in. Next, discrimination, because something ought to be done about those people, after all. Personal attacks follow when discrimination seems too subtle. If isolated attacks won't make those people leave, there's always the ultimate solution—genocide.

Though the forest management controversy never got beyond the fourth level around here (and even that occurred in only a few instances), each step lays the foundation for the next. Not every dog that barks will bite, but no dog bites without barking first.

In Douglas County, I first heard the barking in 1978, during a federal review of potential wilderness areas called RARE II, for Roadless Areas Re-Evaluation, second round.

I was vaguely aware of the controversy and generally in favor of setting aside some of the forest, though I hadn't thought about it much, being busy working fifty hours a week at a local mill. My wife was pregnant and we'd just bought a small place, so my worries were about maintaining my health insurance and making my land payments rather than the health of the forest.

For two months that summer we were urged to oppose wilderness. The foreman shut down the machinery one day to lecture us about the threat that "those goddamn environmentalists" posed to our livelihood, and he offered a free steak dinner for the entire crew if our shift filled out more public comment postcards than any other crew.

I looked at mine, saw that whatever I wrote would be open to my boss's inspection, and tossed it into the chipper feed belt when no one was looking. I wasn't concerned about the politics of forest management, but as a worker I was offended by the postcard.

About a month later I was sent up to the mill-wrights' shop to fetch a gear for one of the machines. When I got there I found the head millwright busily fabricating hatchets, maces, and clubs out of scrap steel. The plant foreman was standing there with him and they were laughing excitedly. I learned that there was to be a public hearing that night at the county fairgrounds on the RARE II review. "We're gonna go out to the fairgrounds and kick ass on them environmentalists," the millwright told me. Nobody was attacked that night, and a week later the weapons were lying in the scrap metal bin without having drawn any blood.

I've often wondered about the millwright and his makeshift weapons. Perhaps he simply thought better of it and left them at the mill. It might be that he and some others actually did bring them to the meeting but changed their minds when confronted with the opportunity to use them. Or maybe they just couldn't pick out anyone to attack because you really can't tell, just by looking, what someone's politics are.

The morning fog seems to magnify sound. Roosters crow at the pale disk of the sun and sound too near, as if the henhouse had somehow moved closer in the night. The familiar view becomes mysterious, the half-seen shapes of trees down by the river float like dark, disembodied autumn spirits.

On fall mornings it's easy to believe in the dream world, that half-guessed realm that lies concealed inside the everyday landscape. Are those brown-cloaked druids filing by in procession or just the neighbor's cows heading out to pasture? What is it about morning fog that turns a telephone pole, mute and alone, its wires connected to mist, into a looming symbol? Which is the real world, this uncertain morning or the day made familiar by sunlight and coffee?

Geese fly by, Canada honkers, in pairs or gaggles, noisily laughing in their awkward flight, joy-filled nomads heading for breakfast in the wheat-stubble fields by the river.

It's hard to stay somber when the honkers fly by. You can't help smiling, listening to their mocking laughter, watching their flailing flight, necks outstretched like sprinters nearing the finish line.

They take their fun seriously, these heavy-bottomed feathered gypsies passing through the valley. "Behold the fowls of the air; for they sow not, neither do they reap, nor gather into barns . . ." And they manage to have a good time of it too.

You seldom see a solitary goose or gander. They seem to know that real fun is sociable. What good is a joke that isn't shared, after all? And they seem to find plenty to laugh at, winging by overhead, trading one-liners like a nightclub filled with comedians, while we stand below, outsiders grinning upward and wondering if the joke just might be on us.

Maybe they do laugh at us earth-bound two-leggeds weighed down with our mortgages and our search for meaning, leading our "lives of quiet desperation" on our lifelong journey from the obstetrics ward to the intensive care unit. The panorama of the human comedy, spread out below, would be enough to amuse generations of those with wings.

Or maybe they just laugh for sheer joy at being geese, delighting in the world spread out like a vast picnic before them, a noisy boisterous tour group passing through, stopping off to enjoy the season before taking wing in great V-shaped flights to other places.

SMALL TOWNS AND QUIET VOICES

It was just a deal that went sour, like so many other schemes that I've hatched over the years. But some things that should have been said, and could have been said, and would have been said, weren't said because of something I said.

It's not as if I made an innocent blunder or got blind-sided by forces beyond my reckoning. I had a hunch speaking up might kill the project and went ahead and took the risk. And who knows, maybe it wouldn't have worked out for other reasons, though it sure seemed like a done deal at the time.

To understand what happened and why requires an understanding of a people and their place, Douglas County, Oregon, "The Timber Capital of the Nation," my home. It's a large rural county, 5,000 square miles of forested mountains with a small, scattered population of 94,000 people. It has a reputation, when people bother to think of it at all, of being a redneck cultural backwater, the home of hillbillies, crackpot secessionists, and Holy Roller revivalism.

While there is some truth to that stereotype, the reality is more complex, as is always the case with stereotypes. Although many of my neighbors, perhaps most, hold views on generalized issues that urban liberals would find appalling, when it comes to the specifics of day-to-day living they are traditionally sweet, honest, and reasonably tolerant people.

Unfortunately, the old-growth timber harvest controversy created some serious problems here. As a citizen and a writer, I tried to help people understand this complex problem and its ramifications. But facts and reason, I learned, are not politically expedient.

The industrial and environmental issues each spawned mass movements with opposing views, and neither group was interested in presenting complexity, which might raise doubts in the minds of their followers.

"We face a long, uphill battle against a relentless foe whose arrogance, lust for power, and disregard for human suffering seem to know no bounds," one pamphleteer wrote regarding the opposition, a statement that could as easily have come from one camp as the other.

The words became flesh and people started getting hurt, first through threats and then by covert actions. Some store owners complained that a "green list" urging customers to boycott their places was circulating. Four of my friends, three environmentalists and an industrial activist, received death threats. Another lost his job. The debate took on the form of harassing phone calls, midnight beer bottles smashed on driveways, a broken windshield, and a note asking, "Who's watching your wife and kids while your [sic] at work?" It was a hidden thing, a painful festering abscess, talked about in private but never mentioned publicly.

I looked for a subtle way to help heal the wound. It seemed to me that we Umpquans were starting to see ourselves and each other as outsiders saw us, as an issue rather than as a people. I was doing some radio and TV commercial voice-over work for a small advertising agency, and I wanted to start up a series of short local-color sketches, which would focus on the things that make us glad we live here.

The idea was to talk about the little things we held in common as a people, the things we all cared about that made up our lives—the landscape; the seasonal cycles of crops and weather; the wild creatures living in our forests, rivers, and fields; and neighborliness. Maybe if we could talk about our everyday lives instead of our fears about the future we'd remember who we were. I wanted to send a flock of sparrows to peck away at a boulder of intolerance.

The agency was enthusiastic and agreed to try to sell the project. They were sure we could get some local business to sponsor it as a radio feature, and I hoped to syndicate a weekly column to local newspapers. I spent

....

two months writing short word-sketches to be called *Upriver Reflections.*

I thought of the project as a series of small hand-painted tiles, each a picture in its own right, forming a large mosaic mural. It was exciting work, and it was both challenging and satisfying to try to get the tone just right—uplifting but not preachy, loving without being schmaltzy, artful but not dishonest.

Two months into the project I was laying the words down and building up material. There were leads on sponsors, a demo tape was planned, and (*mirabile dictu!*) it seemed I would earn a modest steady income while doing something both commercially and socially useful.

But then *The Oregonian* sent some reporters down from Portland for an in-depth series of articles on how the timber controversy was affecting us. It didn't take them long to hear about all the harassment, and soon dozens of people knew that the ugly secret was no longer going to be hidden. The local daily, *The News-Review,* got wind of their inquisitive competitor's plans and a week before *The Oregonian* published its series, the paper did a front page piece exposing what everyone already knew.

I felt relieved, as if a painful boil had finally been lanced. I waited for the public reaction, for an editorial or a public comment from someone suggesting that things had gotten out of hand. But not one local journalist, politician, preacher, educator, or activist spoke

....

up. The only public reaction was a single letter to the editor saying that one of the victims was a traitor who deserved whatever he got.

Since no one spoke out on behalf of the victims, I wrote a guest editorial for the local daily pointing out that intimidation in the name of politics is both shameful and stupid, because preserving the right to express opinions is more important than the outcome of any passing issue.

Nobody publicly agreed or disagreed with me, though several people stopped me on the street or called me on the phone or wrote me letters to thank me for having voiced their own concerns. I didn't get a pipe bomb in my mailbox, but I did get a letter from the advertising agency, concerned that the *Upriver Reflections* project might have to be dropped if I continued to make controversial public statements and they couldn't find any sponsors. As it turned out, the one piece was enough to kill the project.

I understood. It's a small place where everyone knows everyone. In a polarized situation a moderate stance can be highly controversial, and why should a business take risks? It wasn't really censorship or black-listing—I could have pushed it on my own if I'd had the heart. But still, I wonder what effect the project would have had on all of us. I wonder what other calm and quiet things haven't been said or have been drowned out in all the shouting.

THE ENEMY AMONG US OR

THE ENEMY WITHIN US?

"It is easier to love mankind as a whole than to love
one's neighbor."

⌒ Eric Hoffer

Two years ago I was at
Shasta Lake, waiting on a dock with some time to kill,
when I met a woman from Klamath Falls. Since we were
both away from home, our conversation soon turned to
Oregon and the old-growth timber debate between the
environmentalists and the industrialists.

"I don't know what to think," she admitted. "I have
friends who work in the woods and I'd hate to see them
lose their jobs, but I'm worried that the forests really are
being cut too fast too. It's terrible. I keep thinking that
there must be something wrong with me."

"Well, that's normal really," I told her. "It's a tough situation with no easy answers. You *should* be confused and worried because it's a real gut-wrencher. That's healthy. It's the people who don't feel that way who have something wrong with them. Complex problems don't have simple causes or simple solutions. Life just ain't that easy."

Sometimes the ability to see both sides of an issue can be a curse, turning our own hearts into disputed territory, just as the community itself becomes divided. We sometimes yearn for an end to conflicting notions, something comforting we can hang onto that will settle the matter. But this uneasiness, as hard as it is to live with, is unavoidable in a democracy such as ours.

One easy way out of the dilemma is to accept wholly one version or the other of the conflicting views. This simplifies things by reducing matters to two sides instead of many different views. It also brings the comfort of belonging to a group of people who all feel the same way. When an issue, any issue, stirs us up, we can join with others who have a ready-made theory (usually a conspiracy theory aimed at anyone opposed to the group) and escape the discomfort of open-mindedness.

Of course, accepting an "us against them" view doesn't really end our frustration at all. It just gives us a convenient target for it. Reality is a tough and bitter pill to swallow, but sugar-coated lies go down easy. The problem is that reality lingers on after the sugar high fades.

....

Having accepted "arrogant radical preservationists" or "greedy timber barons" as the source of the conflict, we must spend a great deal of energy defending our group's theory against the incursions of reality. The all-too-human desire for an answer we can believe in leads to frustration when the answer we choose is too simple to fit what is actually happening.

Conspiracy theories ignore some basic human traits, such as ignorance, incompetence, and stupidity, to name a few. While these notions are doomed to fail at actually solving anything, they make up for it by providing a target for the frustration they create—"them."

Most of us would rather accept the idea of an enemy among us than examine ourselves for signs of the enemy within each of us. In his remarkable study of fanaticism, *The True Believer*, Eric Hoffer identifies the desire to join a mass movement as the individual's desire to escape from himself. "Blind faith is to a considerable extent a substitute for the lost faith in ourselves," he says. Later he goes on to warn of the consequences of this flight from ourselves: "When we lose our individual independence in the corporateness of a mass movement, we find a new freedom—freedom to hate, bully, lie, torture, murder, and betray without shame or remorse. Herein undoubtedly lies part of the attractiveness of a mass movement."

Douglas County has changed in the last ten years. People are much more fear-filled now than they were. Tolerance used to be a hallmark of life here in the

....

Hundred Valleys of the Umpqua, but now we have become the land of the anonymous death threat, the window broken in the night, the job lost because of political beliefs, and the whispered accusation that turns neighbor against neighbor—a cowardly land of "us and them."

It is a shameful way of life for which we all bear responsibility. We have killed our hearts because we found pain there, the pain of hard choices. What we have left now is something inhuman and heartless. We have learned to hate one another. Because we could not trust ourselves to love, we have given in to fear.

Fearfulness is unavoidable in an open society. If we don't accept the hard struggle it is to live with uncertainty, we'll have to accept the death of openness, accept either Thomas Jefferson or Adolf Hitler, the Bill of Rights or Kristallnacht. Those are the choices we have to make for ourselves, the choices that will determine our future long after the issues of today have faded away.

THE SMELL OF HOME

Upriver from Tiller, Oregon, the South Umpqua River pours through a narrow channel between gray basalt rock faces into a deep, still pool where salmon circle slowly, waiting for fall rains. The spring Chinook arrive here in June after a two-hundred-mile journey upriver from the ocean.

The salmon know the smell of home, the scent of jasper, basalt, porphyry, quartz, agate, and tufa carried by the waters from the gravel bars where they hatched. Patiently they work their way against the current, returning from the Aleutian Islands home to the South Umpqua.

They wait out the long summer months—when the river slows and the water grows warmer—never eating, living on the fat stored in their huge bodies. On summer mornings you can see the sore-head fish from the cliffs above, silvery ghost shapes in the sun-dappled waters below, moving in a slow, solemn circle dance.

They are a bruised and battered lot, bearing the marks of their passage: old wounds from seal bites, fish-hooks, nets, and the scraping of rocks encountered in the riffles of the home stretch. Their flesh, once firm from the arctic feeding grounds, grows soft in the warm river water. Fuzzy white patches appear on their scaly sides, the mark of infection and a sign of approaching death.

They are prisoners here for a while, holding in the deeper pools scattered among the shallow upper reaches of the river, rising in the cool quiet morning hours, and hiding in the depths when the afternoon comes, bringing heat and the campers and bathers who splash about on the surface.

Evening comes, and the humans leave. Blacktail deer come down to drink. The firs and cedars cast long shadows across the pool. The clever-handed raccoons fish for crawdads along the edges, and silence returns to their watery world with the night.

There is a quiet joyfulness to the salmon's languid circling—not the exuberance of their leaping struggle through white water on their way upstream, but a deeper joy made of patience, survival, and expectation. Their long journey is nearly over, the uncounted thousands of miles behind them. Soon the rains will come and they'll swim upriver on the rising waters as their ancestors have always done, to dig their nests on gravel bars and lay their eggs in the waters of home.

The rock is older than the river. Two hundred million years ago it welled up from the floor of a shallow Jurassic sea. Along with a dozen other nearby outcroppings collectively called the Boomer Hill monoliths, it was slowly buried and lost until the Klamath Mountains rose, forming the South Umpqua River. The river cut its way down to the rock and around it, leaving a deep pool at its base. Both the rock and the river are young when reckoned in geologic time. Still, its gray-green face has looked down on those waters for a good long while.

It's a big rock, about twenty feet high and running along the riverbank for a hundred feet, all one solid mass. Every year, about the time when the spring Chinook salmon have finished their migration upriver, I take its measure and my own. So far, I've changed more than it has.

There are many diving spots on the river—cliffs and rocks and bridges—all the way from Deer Lick Falls on the headwaters down to the sea. But Boomer Hill Rock is special for me. It's the closest one to my home, the dive I know best. It's also just the right height—low enough for safety but high enough to frighten me.

At middle age, I find that I scare more easily than I used to. I can remember flinging myself from the rock in drunken, sloppy flips, convinced of my own invulnerability. I no longer expect to live forever, and so I approach the dive, as I try to approach everything these days, with more respect.

The first dive of the season belongs to this place. Often it's the first swim in the river for the year—a brief fall into the joys of summer. My feet are always tender after the cold months. The sand is hot and the rocks are sharp. I could swim upstream to the rock from the beach where we lay out our towels and picnic paraphernalia. My son always sprints into the water here. My wife wades in slowly, inching her way into the cold water until it reaches her shoulders and then gliding away purposefully upstream. But before that first dive I avoid all contact with the river, not out of superstition but from a sense of propriety, a desire to do this one thing right in spite of all the other things in my life that I botch.

From the beach I walk along the riverbank and climb the rock from the back side, cross its top, and come to the edge where a stone, about the size and shape of a football caught in the matrix, juts out over the water. It's not all that high (I've dived from twice that height before), but from on top it looks higher than it really is. The river here is deep, wide, and slow, a stretch where it tries to become a lake. The water is green with gold speckles but clear enough that I can see several feet below the surface, giving the illusion of added height.

There's also an optical phenomenon here, the same one that makes circular rainbows around the shadows of airplanes on the clouds below. When I stand on the rock with the afternoon sun at my back, my shadow on the water has golden rays of light emanating from it. The ancient Hawaiians used to climb to the rim of Haleakala Crater on Maui to see their shadows on the clouds trapped in the caldera below. They called it *akakuanuenue,* "seeing your soul."

I've seen it all many times over the years, the dis-embodied submerged reef forty feet out in the river, the dappled silver and black light on the surface of the water, the golden halo of my shadow, the half-guessed shapes of fish swimming along the reef below. There's a dreamlike state of mind that is brought on by the scene, my own nervousness, and a touch of vertigo. It's impor-tant for practical as well as spiritual reasons to shake it off before I dive.

Looking up helps. Sometimes there are teenagers sitting on the reef or up on top of the rock; sometimes there's just my wife and son, small figures on the beach downstream, looking up at me. I used to work as a steeplejack, facing the fear of falling every day and often at night in my dreams. There are worse fears though, the kind without names that are known only by the chill they produce, more terrible because of their ambiguity.

There's something very simple and clear and honest about cliff diving that appeals to me even more than the thrill. It's hard to find moments like that in this muddled age.

The dive itself is deceptively simple: Spring out, align the body, and fall. I have a friend who teaches kung fu. He told me that breaking bricks with his bare hands feels very relaxing when he does it right. I can believe him, because that's the way a proper dive feels, very natural and effortless. Other than body mechanics, two mistakes can mar a dive—shying away from the water and reaching for it. Both can lead to injury and both are the result of fear. But fear is a projection onto the future, and there's no room here for anything but the task at hand.

I wave to my family, fold my hands in an attitude of prayer, and begin focusing my mind on the dive, imagining it step by step ahead of time: the stretch, the crouch, the springing, aligning my body, falling, and entering the water—Zen archery, with my body as the arrow. And then I do it.

There is a momentary empty feeling in my stomach, the tingle of leg muscles as I crouch and leap, a weightlessness, the sparkle of light, the roar of water in my ears, and a rush of bubbles along my skin as I glide along in the deep, slow down, and then swim up toward the surface.

WHO OWNS THE RIVER?

When my wife and I moved to the Umpqua, a big part of the reason we settled in this valley was the river. We grew up in Los Angeles, and having a river was something new and exciting. Swimming, rafting, and fishing the river or just seeing it out our living room window made us feel like millionaires even though we were barely getting by.

It's easier now to forget just how important the river is to our lives because it is always there, present in just about everything we do. Trying to appreciate it is like trying to appreciate air or sunlight or the roof over our heads or each other.

When our son was seven years old, we flew down to Los Angeles for Christmas. The boy was born in Roseburg, Oregon, and on the flight I was trying to see through his eyes, as fathers do, wondering what he'd think of the overwhelming reality of a major city.

Someday, I knew, he'd grow up and decide for himself whether to live in the small town of his birth or to move.

It's an important question in many ways, both for the family and for the place where we live. The migrations of four generations, from Kazakhstan to North Dakota to California and to Oregon, have allowed our family to survive but left us poorer too, as the miles and the years pile up to cut us off from our past. The valley also suffers when the young leave and the land falls to new people who don't understand its limits. It takes long years of generations living in a place to build both the family and the culture that can allow the place to survive.

Sitting next to my son as we came into Hollywood/Burbank Airport, I watched him looking out the window at the San Fernando Valley below. He pointed toward the Santa Monica Mountains in the west and asked me, "Dad, what's that big gray thing over there?"

"Oh, that's the Ventura Freeway," I told him. "Sure is big, ain't it? Look at all those cars. You never see a freeway that big at home."

"No, Dad," he said, "not the freeway—that thing right next to it, the big concrete thing."

"Oh that. Well, that's the Los Angeles River," I told him, and he looked at me in disbelief. When he realized that I wasn't kidding him, his face contorted in revulsion.

"That's a river?"

"Well, yeah, sort of," I told him, "at least it used to be, but they paved it back before I was born, back when my big brothers were little. It's just a big storm drain now, dumps all the rainwater out to the ocean, but it used to be a real river with fish and trees and all."

The Los Angeles River is a good example of what happens when we see our world as a collection of unrelated things that we can tinker with. What happened to the river also happened to the valley and the people because, in reality, they don't exist as isolated parts but coexist as something much more complex.

The Umpqua River is not a flood channel or a water supply or a source of hydraulic power for generating electricity or a way to get from one place to another or a playground or a fish hatchery. It is first and foremost itself.

We hear talk about conflicting interests in water ownership—recreation, wildlife, irrigation, land values, and economic development. But it's important to remember that these are all human concerns and that the river itself has its own agenda, one that doesn't recognize any mere human needs.

Who owns the Umpqua? State and federal agencies, urban water and sanitation districts, power companies, farmers, home owners, and sportsmen all lay claim to it. But how can anyone really own a river?

Ownership implies control. Have you ever stood by the riverbank during the high water and watched the flood roaring past and seen those huge waves carrying logs and debris? Can anybody own the flood? Who owns the sunlight on the water? Who owns the osprey's flight or the ghostly shapes of spring Chinook salmon circling in deep pools? Who owns the raccoons reaching under rocks for crawdads at night? Who owns the sound of whitewater rapids or the color of maple trees in the fall? They're not yours or mine at all—they belong to the river.

In many ways we've got the whole notion backwards. We don't own the river—the river owns us. We are its people, the people of the Umpqua. Everywhere we go, we are forced to encounter the river. When we give directions we say "upriver" and "downriver" or "across the river" instead of "east" or "west" or "north" or "south."

The river is an inescapable fact of life here. It shapes us even more than we shape it. We need it more than it needs us. It was here before we were, and it will still be here long after we're gone. We can dam it, channelize it, pump water from it, build bridges over it; but in the end, whatever we do is only temporary, because the river will do what it's going to do. It has a strength and a patience that are beyond our own and a wisdom that is beyond our understanding.

At best, we can hope to live in some kind of harmony with the river, but that's only possible if we approach it with a great deal of humility. All of the mistakes we've made, the problems we've created, have come from our arrogance in thinking that somehow we understand the river and can manipulate it for our own purposes.

On Sunday morning, February 16, 1870, the stern-wheeler *Swan* arrived in Roseburg. Within minutes church bells were ringing, people were firing guns into the air, and a wild celebration broke out all over town. It was hailed as the dawn of a new era of economic prosperity for Douglas County.

The boat had come, inching its way upstream from Scottsburg, at the instigation of the Merchants and Farmers Navigation Company, a local group that had formed to open the Umpqua River to steamboat travel.

At the time, the Oregon and California Railroad had halted construction at Eugene, seventy miles north, for lack of funds. The 1,500 tons of goods imported annually into Douglas County and the 1,000 tons of goods being exported were still being hauled in wagons to and from Scottsburg, a long trip that cost $40 per ton in freight charges. A steamboat could carry the freight for half that price, saving $50,000 every year—if a riverboat could force its way upriver to Roseburg.

Captain Haun declared that the river could be made navigable by blasting a handful of obstructions at a cost of a few hundred dollars. The Navigation Company petitioned Congress for a study, and the Army Corps of Engineers sent out a survey party that summer. Despite the fact that the river was impassable even in a rowboat by then, the engineers recommended the project. After all, impossible as it seemed, the *Swan* had made the trip.

Having waved the magic wand of a feasibility study over the project, Congress appropriated $22,500 to make the river navigable—about forty times the amount that Captain Haun had said it would cost. Contractors spent the summer of 1871 blasting ledges and boulders and pulling logs out of the river to carve a boat channel while the Navigation Company built a new riverboat, appropriately christened the *Enterprise*, to make the inaugural run.

When the fall rains came, the *Enterprise* set out from Scottsburg. Unfortunately, it never arrived in Roseburg. The new channel had sped up the current and the boat couldn't fight the increased flow. Even if the *Enterprise* had reached town, it was too late by then anyway. In April of 1872, a few months after the new riverboat's unsuccessful maiden voyage, the O&C Railroad line reached Roseburg, making steamboat travel obsolete.

The Merchants and Farmers Navigation Company folded in 1872, three years after it began, but the steamboat channel is still there, and we're still paying for it. For the past 120 years the river has flowed more swiftly, causing greater winter erosion and lower summer water tables. When we look at the consequences of an increased water flow rate—less water storage, more soil erosion, loss of riparian vegetation, siltation, warmer and more polluted water, fewer fish it's a safe bet that the true cost of the riverboat project has been millions of dollars.

It takes a long time to understand a place, to learn what its limits are. The beaver were trapped out between 1820 and 1840 and with them went the thousands of small dams they built. Hydraulic gold mining silted up hundreds of miles of gravel spawning beds. Moving logs downriver scoured the bottom. Marshes were drained to make pasture. Cattle and sheep grazed off the streamside brush, causing erosion as the banks gave out. Clear-cutting removed thousands of acres of the forest canopy. Following the flood of 1964, the federal government began a program aimed at removing woody debris from the headwaters creeks, turning them into what might as well be concrete storm drains.

All these practices have changed the dynamics of the river. We have always had about the same amount of rainfall, but what has changed is what happens to the water. It gets to the ocean much more quickly now, instead of soaking into the soil and spreading out. Lower summer flows, coupled with less shade from trees and brush, make for warmer water. Pumping water out for urban water systems and farm irrigation leaves what's left lower and warmer and funkier still. Pollution from industrial chemicals, sewage spills, and agricultural runoffs becomes even more disastrous when there's less water to dilute it.

It's hard to see the changes happening because the damage hasn't been a matter of dramatic calamities. Instead, it has occurred slowly, bit by bit over the past 150 years—a wetland drained here, a grove of trees logged off there, a road cut too close to a stream, a field that has been overgrazed. None of these small events, in and of themselves, is enough to kill a river. But the accumulation of these misuses, over a period of time spanning several generations, amounts to a disaster greater than any flood or wildfire or chemical spill.

If we could see it happening all at once, we'd be much more alarmed. Rust and fire are the same chemical process—oxidation. If your car was in flames you'd call the fire department. But it's easy to ignore rust, even though it'll ruin the car just as surely and completely as a fire, given enough time. It's the same process, the only difference being a matter of pace.

The river's pace is not a human one. Our longest personal measurement, our own life span, is barely enough to begin measuring the rate of change in a river. And, of course, even that requires careful attention, decades of accurate observation.

Our home in Myrtle Creek sits up on a hillside, about 150 feet above the valley floor. From our living room we can look out across the Missouri Bottoms, a small alluvial plain about a half-mile wide and four miles long. The South Umpqua River runs through the valley, and so does Interstate 5, the Southern Pacific's Siskiyou Line, and Old Highway 99. It's the only flat ground for miles around.

The valley used to be called Orchard Valley because it was planted in prunes, back before refrigeration killed off the dried-fruit industry. The orchards are pretty much gone now, with just a few patches remaining here and there, but the bottoms are still farmland, with wheat, hay, and pastures. It's prime land, loamy top soil anywhere from twelve to thirty feet deep.

The bottomlands look flat but aren't really. When the sun gets low in the late afternoon you can see the shadows cast by a network of gentle swales winding through the Missouri Bottoms, running in the same direction as the river.

It took me a year of living up on the hill above before I noticed them. It's a subtle thing, and even when I did notice them I never paid them much attention. I assumed that they were the remains of old river channels, carved out as the lifting of the mountains on either side of the valley pushed the river back and forth between them.

One morning, after I'd lived on the place for five years, I went out to the barn to milk our cow and heard a roaring sound. It was dark out, wintertime, and it had been raining hard all night. I figured that the noise was from Hilp Creek, running through my place a hundred yards from the barn.

I sat on my stool, milking the cow, and as the sun came up, I was able to see out across the valley and realized what was going on. The river had jumped its banks. The high water was running through the bottoms. A whole new river was running parallel to the main channel and all across the bottoms the swales were full of brown water, smaller rivers intertwining and feeding into the two main flows.

The words "flood plain" came to me and with them an explanation for the swales: flood channels cut by the high water. I thought I understood now how the bottoms were formed. But it wasn't until four years later that, almost by accident, I finally learned the truth.

I was interviewing a fisheries biologist for the Forest Service. While telling me about salmon and steelhead habitat improvement projects up Steamboat Creek, he mentioned that the Willamette River, which runs in a single channel today, used to be a braided stream. In the stretch between Eugene and Corvallis the river ran all year round through a network of nine to eleven major channels, with many side sloughs.

The Willamette Valley was a vast wetland, with beaver ponds, marshes, and islands between the main channels. Flooding was an annual event. The river channels were choked with debris, which slowed down the river current and spread it out, allowing the soil washing down from the mountains to settle out and build up. The marshes were home to huge flocks of geese and ducks. Thousands of herons and cranes and swans, osprey and eagles lived there. Fish and amphibians and insects provided food.

The Missouri Bottoms below my house must have been a smaller version of the same sort of marsh. For years I'd looked out over that land, but it never occurred to me that the river used to run all year round through several shallow channels.

Several things suddenly made sense to me. Old Highway 99 runs along the hillside on the opposite side of the valley. I knew that it followed the old Applegate Trail and that the pioneer trail followed the Indian trade route, but why did it go up on the hillside instead of through the flatter bottoms where the freeway runs? Because the bottom was a swamp—you couldn't walk through there, let alone drive a wagon through it.

I understood how thirty feet of topsoil had built up. A single channel would never have slowed down enough to leave that silt behind, but a marsh, one that became a seasonal lake every spring, would.

I recalled passages from settlers' diaries that mentioned the huge flocks of waterfowl, so thick that to hunt them, they simply startled the birds into flight and fired randomly into the air, bringing down ducks and geese with every shotgun blast. Where had these uncountable thousands of birds lived and why weren't they around anymore?

The South Umpqua, as we see it now, a single channel with banks twenty to thirty feet high, is a modern creation. The marsh was drained for farmland, forcing the water into a single channel, which flowed faster and cut its way down through the soil to bedrock.

What's the effect of that? For one thing, the soil eroded from the mountains no longer settles in the valley; it washes downriver to Reedsport, where the Army Corps of Engineers dredges it out to keep a navigation channel open.

The wetlands used to store water and did it much more efficiently than any dam because the water was stored in the soil, keeping the groundwater table higher. Along with storage the marsh provided filtration and cooling, so not only is there less water now, but what we have isn't as cool and clean as it used to be.

Of course, we've lost the wildlife habitat too. Wetlands are tremendously productive. In order to make wheat fields and hay ground and pasture, we've drained our wetlands, but in terms of sheer protein per acre, the "dismal swamps" were much more productive than the farmland that replaced them.

Someday we may decide to restore the marsh. We may decide that the benefits of erosion control, flood control, water storage and filtration, and wildlife enhancement outweigh the value of the crops that the land produces.

～

The San Fernando Valley, down in Los Angeles, is also an alluvial plain. Although they've built a city on it, the essential nature of the place hasn't changed. It's still a catch basin for the runoff from the surrounding mountains, and every once in a while nature reminds them of that fact with a flood.

Back around the turn of the century, Los Angeles County was the top farming county in California. I can still remember driving through the San Fernando Valley as a child and seeing farmers working their fields while housing projects were springing up all around them. My father once told me about coming to Los Angeles in the 1930s. He used to hunt ducks and geese in the marshes of the San Fernando Valley. The old nickname for the valley was "The Frog Pond," and people still call it that sometimes.

To see the place now, it's hard to imagine how it was when waterfowl wintered there and condors still soared above the hills. But the change came in a single generation, in the thirty years between my father's early manhood and my own.

My father came to a place of beauty to start a family because his birthplace couldn't provide a decent living. I had to do the same thing because my birthplace had become a wasteland of concrete and asphalt and smog and crime. I'm hoping that my son won't have to do it all over again, that maybe this time we've found a place that will stay beautiful and safe.

It's hard to say whether that will happen or not. Dangerous changes come, sometimes unexpectedly and sometimes slowly. But if this place is to survive, the Umpqua River, the living heart of these valleys, needs to be watched over and cared for so it can continue to take care of us, its people.

Nothing seems more permanent here than the mountains, the strong rib cages of the Umpqua Valleys. Rising steeply from the bottomlands along the river, they stand fixed with a patience beyond time, a reminder of just how short the days of the men and women below really are. Their forested slopes, the grazing ground of clouds, draw our eyes upward and remind us of things beyond our knowing, of the secrets hidden in their distant blue folds.

And yet the mountains move. They are alive, growing and changing in their own time, so slowly that usually only the most exact instruments can measure their pace.

But sometimes in winter the warm rains come, melting the high-country snow. Then the mountains move swiftly in the night, and we awake to marvel at the suddenness of change.

The roadside culverts spew their ditch water, rivulets turn to streams, creeks become rivers, and the gentle river rises brown and huge, transformed overnight into great roaring high-water creatures that claw at their banks as the mountainsides slip down to the valleys.

In grains of sand and clay, in pebbles and rocks, boulders and trees, the mountains come down on the flood.

We wake and watch, filled with uncertainty, our own lives no longer fixed and stable when the mountains move. We listen to reports and call our neighbors, trying to find something to cling to in the news of washouts and road closings, weather predictions and warnings. We go out to find our familiar places changed beyond recognition. Finally, we accept the fact that we are caught in something beyond our knowing or control, and fear gives way to elation.

The unexpected event forces us to cancel our routines for a while, and a carnival air comes with the impromptu holiday. No work. No school. Nothing to do but wait and see what it will bring. All our plans are dwarfed by the giant among us.

We come out to see the whirling waters, to gather along the overrun banks and watch the foaming mats of debris riding swiftly to the sea. Logs shoot through high crested waves, railroad ties and pump houses fly past. Bits and pieces of cast-off trash become oddly significant as they bobble past the small groups of people on the shore. Old-timers watch and nod and compare the high water with floods in the past. For a change they are listened to attentively as they assure their audiences that they've seen much, much worse.

ANIMALS

The boy was pumped this morning on the ride to school. My son has his first game today—the Coffenberry Junior High Hornets vs. the John C. Fremont Junior High Generals. He's on the Coffenberry seventh grade football team, playing first-string offensive tackle, second-string linebacker, and blocking on the kick-return squad. The coaches told the boys to wear their jerseys to school today so the kids could "see who the studs are."

He was sitting there, wearing his black jersey with the gold #79, muttering "We're gonna kill 'em," with this wild look in his eye. I could tell he was worried about the game too, going up against a big city team. "We gotta beat 'em."

To my amazement he weighed in at 4'11" and 122 pounds at his physical—I didn't weigh that much until I was eighteen or nineteen. But he has lost some gut in the last three weeks, down to 118.

"Jeeze, Dad, they ran us 'til we almost puked."

"Yeah, how 'bout that? Who would've imagined?" I'd been telling Kurt all summer to get in shape, repeating ominously, "Hell Week's coming, son—you'd better be ready." But I don't think he really believed me.

It never occurred to me that I'd be the father of a football player. My brothers all grew to be short and stout like my father and grandfather, but I was the runt of the litter, short and skinny. As a 104-pound fourteen-year-old who was better at writing sonnets than sacking quarterbacks, I suffered through a season of Physical Education touch football with the nickname of "Animal," as in: "Okay, so that leaves us with Animal, so you guys have to kick off and we receive."

Coach Fred was the head football coach at my high school, and I still shudder at the memory of having him for our PE teacher. "There's only two kinds of kids here," he told us on the first day of our freshman year. "There's the Studs and the Duds. The Studs play football and they don't have to work out in this class. The rest of you are all Duds and you're going to wish you were dead."

He worked us unmercifully, and as the school's premiere football season went on, piling up loss after loss, we duds came in for increasingly harsher treatment: push-ups and sit-ups in the muddiest part of the field and endless miles of running.

The coach's favorite target was a friend of mine named Jan Mankowski, a burly kid with biceps bigger than my thighs. I made the mistake of lining up opposite Jan one day during a PE touch football game. He knocked me a full five yards, from one chalk line to the next, airborne every inch of the way. Coach Fred had spotted him in the hallway on the first day of school and immediately tried to recruit him. "Forget it," Jan told him. "Football's stupid. I'm going out for shot put."

One of my older brothers played four years of high school football, breaking each of his ankles twice. Years later, in a beery middle-aged conversation, I asked him about those days, whether it was worth it to go through all those injuries.

"Oh, it was great!" he said. "I couldn't believe it. I felt like, 'Wow, you mean I get to run around and smash into people and not get in trouble for it? All right!' The coaches loved me. I was in heaven."

Last spring I was coaching first base for my son's Little League team, and Kurt got tagged out coming into home plate. I could see him muttering darkly in the dugout, so when he took the field for the bottom of the inning, I called him aside. I explained to him that it was the manager's mistake, that he should have been held up at third, but he took the routine play as a personal affront and was mad at the catcher for tagging him.

"I'm gonna get him," he was muttering.

Two innings later, he came into the plate low and sideways, a perfect body block, knocked the catcher for a loop, and scored a run. The umpire should have called him out, since Little League rules wisely require runners to slide in that situation, but the ump blew the call and Kurt strutted to the dugout amid parental cheers and high fives from his teammates.

I called him over to my coach's box and, struggling to keep a straight face, chewed him out. "That was a Major League play, son, but this is Little League and you can't do that—even in high school ball you have to slide. You should have been called out."

"Yeah, I know," he said, "but I just wanted to cream him so bad."

"Well, don't ever do it again. Somebody could have been hurt."

"Okay," he reluctantly agreed, "but it sure felt good."

Later, on the ride home from the game, he confessed, "You know, Dad, I like baseball and all, but I think football's really my game."

I picked him up at football practice the other day, the first time that I saw him suited up. Most of the kids look like kids, skinny arms and narrow shoulders with pads that stick out too far, but Kurt looks like an honest-to-God football player scaled down.

He was walking down from the field with two of his buddies, all sweaty and tired from practicing in the 100-degree heat, the last ones in. A lanky, mildly retarded-looking hillbilly, about eighteen or nineteen, walked by and jokingly told them to hustle.

"Why don't *you* hustle?" one of the boys asked as the young man walked off.

"Who, me?" he shot back.

"We *been* hustling."

"Yeah," added one of the kids after the lanky one had gotten a good forty feet farther up the hill, "why don't you come down here where I can hit you?"

"What'd you say?" The young man turned around and started stomping toward them. I guess they must have felt pretty big in their pads, but they suddenly looked pretty small with this gaunt, snaggly-toothed six-footer coming at them.

They tried to walk off, but he kept bearing down on them, so I yelled over to Kurt, "Hey Kurt-o!" just to let the guy know I was there watching.

"Yeah, Dad?"

"I'm picking you up today. Meet me up here. Okay?"

"Okay."

I didn't get out of the truck, just sat there watching and ready and hoping this guy wasn't a speed freak or some other kind of maniac. But it was one of those

"What'd you say?" "Oh yeah?" "You watch your mouth, kid" kind of confrontations, like house cats hissing and puffing up until somebody backs down and slinks away.

The boys slouched off to the locker room and the hillbilly stopped by the truck on his way back up the hill. His face was thin, with acne scars and Elvis sideburns. He looked like one of those perverts whose mug shots you see in the newspapers.

"Punk kids," he offered by way of explanation. "Somebody's gotta teach 'em some respect," which was true.

"I reckon," I offered, wondering how much self-respect a guy could have if he feels threatened by twelve-year-old kids.

He lit a cigarette. "You want one?"

"No."

"Fuckin' punks," he repeated and walked off scowling.

I sat there in the truck thinking about growing up and testosterone and puberty and the mating battles of bull elk and remembering my father, surrounded by his sons, watching TV through a cloud of cigar smoke as the Los Angeles Rams butted heads with the Green Bay Packers.

I thought about how all-important learning to be a hard-ass once seemed and how glad I was that those days are long past for me. It's probably a good thing the boy doesn't know what's ahead for him, I decided.

Kurt came up from the showers and got in the truck. "How'd practice go?" I asked.

"Great," he said. "We scrimmaged against the eighth graders. I thought they'd be tough, but it was easy. We killed 'em. They're a bunch of wusses. I didn't let one guy get by me."

THE FIELD OF REALITY

The sportswriter for the big-city paper sat in the press box all weekend long mouthing it: "ROSE-burg"—like that, with 90-weight contempt in his voice and a sneer on his face. It got on my nerves real quick.

It got to where I wanted to cold-cock him with a whiskey bottle, but all I had was a can of pop—and that just wouldn't have been right. I mean, if you're going to do something like that, you need the proper tool.

I ought to be used to it by now. I've lived in this place for just shy of twenty years now, and I've been hearing that tone of voice whenever I leave the county. I know what they're thinking when they say it like that: ROSE-burg RED-neck.

Yeah, well, okay, redneck country I guess, for lack of anything better to call it. I won't deny that. But here we were, sitting in one of the finest amateur ballparks in America, watching the 1993 American Legion World

Series unfold below us, and it never occurred to him to wonder why 120 of the most gifted young baseball players in the country were competing for a national championship in a little backwater town like Roseburg.

Three cities currently host the American Legion World Series, all of them small and not noted for much of anything else: Roseburg, Oregon; Fargo, North Dakota; and Boyertown, Pennsylvania. Roseburg, naturally, I know well. As for Fargo, I've never been there, but my folks come from North Dakota, so I can imagine it easily, the type of people who live there and what they do to earn a living and pass the time.

Boyertown is a mystery to me, though it must be small because it's hard to find a map with Boyertown on it. In some ways, at least, it's probably like the other two towns—small, nothing much to do, a place where most of the inhabitants know each other by sight if not by name.

So why has the American Legion picked these little places to host their national championship tournament? Is the Legion itself essentially redneck?

I must admit that the phrase "100 percent Americanism" that adorns their statement of purpose puzzles me. How do you quantify being an American? By what standard of measure? Is is possible to be less than 100 percent Americanistic—say, 92 percent or 73.5 percent—and therefore unacceptable?

The phrase brings to mind the sort of mentality that, during the hysteria of World War I, forbade my sod-busting ancestors from speaking their *muddersproch* in public assembly, both here on the Great Plains of America and on the steppes of the Ukraine (where the goal was probably "100 percent Russianism").

But it has been a long time since the days when Legionnaires lurked in dark alleyways outside union halls, ax handles in hand, waiting to pounce on Wobbly agitators. None of the smiling old men at the tournament seemed capable of anything more violent than a bit of mild ribbing directed at one of their gray-haired buddies. The phrase "100 percent Americanism" seems to be an awkward anachronism, a leftover slogan from a less sophisticated age, and I never heard anyone actually utter it during the long weekend.

So the question remains: why hold their biggest tournament, the national championship for a system of some 4,400 amateur baseball teams, in a little place like Roseburg, Oregon?

Glancing through the record book in my press packet, I found a clue. Between 1925 and 1954 overall attendance at the American Legion World Series tournaments topped 40,000 fans six times but never got that high again.

Since 1955 it has reached over 30,000 ticket sales six times: 1974 and 1993 in Roseburg, Oregon; 1976 and 1977 in Manchester, New Hampshire; 1982 in Boyertown, Pennsylvania; and 1990 in Corvallis, Oregon. The 1993 series attendance reached 34,306— the highest of the six—and had Medford, Oregon, won the final game of the regional tournament in Billings, Montana, instead of losing by a score of four to two, it might have topped 40,000.

Roseburg, Manchester, Boyertown, Corvallis—not exactly what you might call teeming metropolises.

More telling, though, were the attendance records from the two series held in New Orleans: 8,438 fans at a single game in 1937, tenth highest on the list; 374 at a game in 1984, the lowest turnout ever.

The 1937 series in New Orleans drew a total of 22,726 fans, but when it returned there in 1984, only 7,765 bothered to come out to watch the games—fewer patrons for the whole series than had come to a single game forty-seven years before. Somewhere between 1937 and 1984, the city of New Orleans (along with the rest of urban America) let baseball die.

The decline of Major League Baseball (and you will find no one who knows and loves the game who will tell you that it hasn't decayed considerably) was preceded by the decline of amateur baseball. Oh sure, the numbers look good: more kids than ever playing in more leagues, more money spent on more equipment, more and better fields these days. And yet, a whole generation of kids is growing up who've never played unorganized sandlot ball. It's not a matter of numbers and dollars but of something no Certified Public Accountant could show on a spread sheet—love of the game.

My colleague didn't know it, but down below us, watching every game, was old Frosty Loghry. Each day Frosty sat surrounded by a different set of middle-aged men, all of whom had played for him at one time or another. In forty-plus years he has raised two entire generations of young ballplayers who went on to become coaches and umpires, league presidents and commissioners, and, of course, the fathers themselves of young pitchers and catchers and fielders, kids who play for the same teams on the same fields as their fathers and grandfathers before them.

I don't think that happens in Portland or Seattle much. If Portland had a sense of tradition like that, would they let the Beavers, the last of the old Pacific Coast League teams, move to Salt Lake City? And Seattle? Well, the less said about the Mariners' troubles drawing a crowd the better, I guess.

Every day I stopped by and shook Frosty's hand on my way up the stairs to the press box. His guests over the weekend were a *Who's Who* list of Douglas County baseball.

"Well, Frosty, I see you been keeping your bench plenty full," I kidded him one night.

"Well," he confided, "they keep me warm."

Of course, the high-toned sportswriter didn't know who Frosty was or anybody else around here. He didn't recognize Bill Gray, the tournament director, either, because he looked right past him like he wasn't there while Bill was emptying out the wastepaper basket in the press box on Sunday afternoon.

"Hell, Bill, they got you doing everything around here, don't they?" I prodded him.

"Yeah, well, I saw it was full," he explained, a little embarrassed to be caught in the act, and then he grinned and winked at me. "Besides, we want to keep you media types happy, you know. A little good press never hurts, after all."

Seventy-two years old, in poor health, literally risking his life to bring the series to town and run the tournament, and he was up there emptying the trash to keep us comfortable. He was enjoying himself too, you could tell.

I'd done an interview with Bill Gray a few weeks before. He didn't talk much about his health, except to admit that it wasn't as good anymore as it used to be. He talked instead of the sixty-eight-year history of Umpqua Post No. 16 baseball and his own thirty-three years as a commissioner.

Sitting there in the shaded stands behind home plate, looking out across the sunlit field, he talked about the work that had gone into the facility over the years, about the truckers who hauled in crushed pumice for the warning track all the way from Windigo Pass, ninety miles upriver, and were paid in pizzas and beer.

He talked about the new restrooms that volunteers had put in at one quarter of the contractor's bid. He reminisced about getting six hundred old seats from Balboa Stadium, home of the Pacific Coast League Padres in San Diego, when the park was torn down. He talked of lumber, paint, lights, and groundskeeper's carts, and how, through all the years, he'd never been turned down whenever he asked for something.

"But that's kind of how this whole thing has come together," he said. "It's been a work of love by a lot of people, and a lot of interest. It's a good baseball community. We sit down here by ourselves and we support that which we have."

❧

The fact is, despite all our many peculiarly Umpquan faults, this is great baseball country. For one thing, redneck kids, the sons of miners, ranchers, farmers, loggers, and lumber mill workers, make good ball players. For another, it takes a special kind of place full of the right kind of people to keep the game alive generation after generation.

American Legion Baseball in Douglas County is as old as the national program itself. Umpqua Post No. 16 has kept it in continuous operation since 1925. The post runs three single-A teams and one AA team—the Dr. Stewarts, known as the Docs. It costs about $80,000 per season to maintain all four teams, and none of the American Legion posts in any of America's largest cities supports a program of that size.

Season tickets for the six hundred reserved seats that come here from San Diego are sold out every year. To get one you have to wait for someone to die.

According to the program book, which Helen Lesh (season ticket holder since 1953) put together, the Docs won 1,469 games and lost 524 between 1954 and 1991—a .737 win-loss average over thirty-eight seasons, including state and national playoffs, regional tournaments, and world series play.

Everywhere I went that weekend, I was talking to local baseball people, good old boys and girls, working hard with rakes and mops and toilet plungers and having a good old time. It would be easy to go on and on with examples of how hard everyone worked to bring the series here and to stage it, to go on and on about what a remarkable place this is. But falling into some schmaltzy "Field of Dreams" hyperbole would be just plain wrong. What I found was better than any dream—it was a field of reality, with all the unexpected beauty and grittiness of everyday life.

Maybe baseball itself is inherently redneck, or at least something that requires an old-fashioned, unsophisticated way of living that began dying out in most of America during the postwar boom years of the Eisenhower administration and lingers on only in backwater towns.

The thirty years following the Second World War brought a shift in American demographics. We are no longer a rural society with a large blue-collar work force in the cities. Instead, we've largely become a nation of white-collar urban and suburban people.

Of course, many of the old-time values are best left to oblivion. We can't afford racism, sexism, authoritarianism, and nationalism anymore (not that we ever could). But we still haven't managed to replace those social controls with anything more useful and humane, so the future remains in doubt.

Will the Information Age produce good ballplayers? Will the Nintendo generation forsake the honest dirt and grass fields for the video screen simulcrum? Who can say? "It ain't over 'til it's over," as one of the game's wisest men once said. But maybe baseball, like the family farm, is part of a nineteenth-century way of living and, as such, doomed to continue fading away as we enter the twenty-first century.

That the Umpqua is remarkably good baseball country is really a very sad thing—for the game and for the nation. For nearly one hundred years, every town in America had a local team, which was as important to the town as the church or the saloon or the bank. These amateur and semipro teams kept alive local community and family baseball traditions. Many Major League players can trace their baseball roots to one or more of those teams. My cousin, Mark Holzemer, who pitched his first game in the majors that weekend, is one of them.

During the thirties and forties and up until the early fifties, Amidon, North Dakota, the county seat of Slope County, had a population of about 120 people. The town had a team of farm boys and young men, the Amidon Rangers, who played against neighboring towns, upholding the town's reputation for good baseball. My uncle Bud Holzemer played third base, his brother Red played first, and my father filled in occasionally in the outfield.

These young men, who played amid the wheat fields, went on to become the fathers of dozens of young ballplayers and, eventually, the grandparents of even more.

The Amidon Rangers played their last game in 1953, at about the same time when American Legion World Series attendance began dropping off. People moved away, unable to scratch out a living, and the demise of the town's team came early on in that decline. Today, Amidon's population numbers twenty-nine souls.

We have a long tradition of talking about the curative powers of baseball. Writers and baseball officials often speak of it in the sort of mystical terms that medieval alchemists used in portraying the panacea, the universal remedy that would cure all mortal afflictions. The American Legion's National Americanism Commission falls squarely within this tradition. The program will, we are told, "combat juvenile delinquency," "build our nation's future," and help develop "a feeling of citizenship, sportsmanship, loyalty, and team spirit."

But the game really doesn't need justification at all. Ennobling it with lofty claims of social benefit is really a disservice. The primary reason the game caught on and has survived is that it's a hell of a lot of fun to watch and play baseball—though you'd never suspect that from a reading of the program's purpose and goals.

Such talk misses the point in another way. Though the game can certainly help the community, it cannot survive without the community's support. Baseball can only pay back what's given to it.

Ecologists talk of "indicator species," creatures like the northern spotted owl, whose rise and fall in population are a measure of the overall health of the ecosystems without which they cannot survive. Baseball, and especially amateur baseball, its purest form, is an indicator of a community's health.

The number of communities that support a strong amateur baseball program—not just with dollars but by passing along knowledge and, above all else, love for the game—is a measure of the nation's health. When baseball dies out in a community it means that there is no community there anymore, just a place with a name, some fixed boundaries, and a rootless, fragmented population.

NIÑOS

Ashley had something she wanted to tell me. All the other kids were hurrying out the classroom door for free play, but she came over and looked up at me with her four-year-old "I've got a secret" eyes.

"What's up, honey?"

She beckoned with her finger, and I lowered my ear to her. "I love you," she whispered, then she looked me in the eyes, smiled, and scurried out the door.

It was springtime outside. Sunlight and the laughter of children at play filtered through the venetian blinds and poured in through the open door. I straightened up and stood for a moment, caught in the present, overcome by joy and humility, and wondrously alive again.

I tell stories to kids (and big folks too—when they'll listen). Witches and wise women, wicked wolves and wily coyotes, dragons, treasures, and the Land of Faery are my stock in trade, but I was overwhelmed by a bit of real magic more potent than anything in my tales.

It wasn't the first time that a little one had done that. I work with two local Head Start classes of four- and five-year-olds. The kids are mostly from poor families. Many of them have no men in their lives, a need that almost smothers me at times as they cling to my hands and crowd into my lap during my weekly visits.

At times it's painful for me to know these children and care about them, realizing that, in the end, they're someone else's kids. Some of them carry an unconscious weight about them, the heaviness of defeat learned before their ABCs. A friend of mine, who says he sees auras, describes it as a cloudiness obscuring their luminescence. I don't have the knack of seeing souls, but there's something about the notion of children as small orbiting suns that appeals to me and something painful in the thought of their glow being eclipsed by the larger, denser planets of us big folks.

Every year, when Halloween is approaching, I tell a Shasta story about a man who journeys to the Land of the Dead to fetch his wife back to the village. He lacks the strength to carry her home and fails in his quest, dies himself, and is reunited with her in death. It is a sad story, of course, as any good story about grief must be.

One year, after I'd told the story to a classroom of second graders, Misty came up to me and told me her own tale: "The night when my grandpa died, Mama drank a whole bottle of schnapps and she passed out. My dad had to put her to bed. In the morning, the ambulance men came to take Grandpa away, and I saw them carrying him out."

She told it so simply and quietly that I was a little stunned. For a moment I just sat there, seeing the knowledge of grief in her eyes and searching for a reply. I could picture it all: the old man a sudden corpse in the bedroom, her mother's tears, her father tenderly carrying her mother off to sodden slumber, the strangers with their gurney arriving in the morning, and the little girl watching it all in wonderment. What can you say to a child who has confronted the mystery of mortality like that?

It's tough sometimes, not knowing really what to say to a child. They expect wisdom that we grown-ups don't always have. The stories contain great wisdom, but the teller is generally just as foolish as everyone else.

Children seldom see the "quiet desperation" that underlies adult life. Of course, we try to conceal it from them out of a mixed desire to protect them from uncertainty and to protect ourselves from insecurity, because, despite our posturing, we're just as confused about life as they are.

I said the conventional things. I told her about my own father's death and that death is natural, just something we all go through, and that people don't really die because we remember them. "Mama says Grandpa's in Heaven with the angels and he's happy," she told me. And though I don't really believe in pearly gates and streets paved with gold or everlasting hellfire and brim-stone, I told her that her mother was right.

Looking back on it, I'm not sure whether she needed reassurance or just a chance to talk about death, something we don't talk about as a rule. Either way, she seemed relieved—almost as relieved as I was.

Several years ago, when I first began telling stories, one class had a mildly retarded five-year-old boy named Arlen, who glommed onto me right away. After a few weeks, I met his mother, who had the same distracted, fogbound look in her eyes. I wrote his behavior off to genetics and the odd way that kids, dogs, drunks, women in trouble, and crazy people always seem to be attracted to me. But talking to his teacher, I learned that his father had flung him against a wall during an infant crying fit, permanently damaging his brain.

One day he pulled me aside and whispered, "I'm the only one who loves you, Bob." It was an eerie moment. He said it with such sincerity that I half-suspected he was right. I laughed, a little embarrassed, and thanked him, thinking that he was trying to get some attention by conning me. I assumed that he meant, "These other

kids are just jiving you, but I'm the only one here who
really loves you, so ignore them and pay attention only
to me." Later though, I read an interview with Alice
Miller, a Swiss psychologist who studies child abuse,
and I wondered if he was really saying, "You're the only
one who loves me."

CENTRAL HEAT

Ｗe can count ourselves lucky that so many ways of doing things that are obsolete elsewhere linger on here. We may be part of the twentieth century, but we understand the older pace too, the slower rhythms of a life that moves to the long cycles of nature. Umpqua kids understand the old characters in fairy tales; goats and foxes and ravens don't need to be explained. Old clichés such as "making hay while the sun shines" or "a tough row to hoe" are still self-evident and very much alive for us.

One of those old-time phrases that still makes sense locally (though it has died out for most Americans) is "hearth and home." I've heard city folks pronounce it "*heart* and home," and though they may not know what a hearth is, they're really not too far from the truth.

From the first morning cup of coffee to the final light-switch tour at night, we keep checking on the wood-burning stove. We listen to the roar of newspaper, junk mail, and kindling and wait for the sound that says it's time for cordwood. We adjust the damper and add pieces at the right time to keep the fire just right—hot enough to burn clean, slow enough to last. Like the family itself, it takes care and patience and skill to provide warmth without too much heat.

With every trip to the firewood pile, we take stock of our stored warmth, counting the days till spring piece by piece, secure and complacent or worried, depending on the height of stacked rows of madrone, oak, maple, fir, and cedar. The pieces sound like baseball bats as we load them in our arms, and when we return, the faint smell of smoke greets us at the door.

The old woodburner sits in the living room and draws us irresistibly to it on winter mornings. Even the cat can't resist and lies sleeping nearby all day. As we go about our busy day, we keep returning to the same spot, over and over again, like comets returning to the sun after traveling the long cold void of space.

We stand and stretch out our hands toward the warm iron and steel and turn slowly from front to back, absorbing warmth and comfort and, perhaps, a bit of courage too. It's a cold world out there, after all, and nothing helps chase away the damp like the glowing heart of home.

EDGAR AND THE CLUSTER

It was December and a time of bad news, and I was waiting for my son's school bus. The bus won't come to the house anymore. Our little gravel road is too narrow and winding to be safe, they say, and there's the school budget cuts, of course, so he gets dropped off a mile north at old George Roy's driveway at a quarter after three.

When my son was five, his main ambition in life (except for wearing a cape and leaping tall buildings in a single bound) was to ride the school bus like the big kids. Now, at thirteen, he gets suspended from the bus for rowdiness once or twice a year and wants to be seven feet tall so he can slam-dunk a basketball.

I was early and sat in Edgar waiting for the bus. Edgar Alan Datsun needs a new pair of front tires, a tune-up, a fuel filter, and a new clutch. But it's a hard time of year to come up with extra money. Oh well, the small get by; to keep under is to endure. The old flap-fender pickup will undoubtedly keep running. In the eight years and uncountable (no odometer) miles since I inherited him, Edgar the Haunted Truck has never quite given up the ghost.

He's a benevolent ghost, named Steve, and I'd hate to lose him since he's been a great comfort to me over the years, though at first I was a little leery of him. For four years, before Steve Hoeffler snuffed himself breathing exhaust fumes in Edgar's cab, he and I were friends. So when his brother and sister showed up from California to dispose of his bright-red corpse, they gave me his pickup.

It was awkward at first, accepting such a grim legacy, and I almost refused. But we were broke at the time and couldn't afford to be too proud. White Man's Burden, my 1961 GMC, only got eight miles to the gallon with its monster V-6 engine, so getting one of those little Japanese rigs for free and selling off the Gemmy was just too good to pass up.

Edgar was running rough when I got him, and when I discovered that one of the spark plugs was defunct, I laughed and shook my head, saying out loud, "Steve, you dumb-ass motherfucker, you were only running on three cylinders." It was the first time I'd spoken to him since he'd died, and I felt better.

~

I dreamed I saw Steve Hoeffler one night—alive as you or me. He was sitting in my living room, quiet as usual, but clearly enjoying himself. I knew he wasn't

....

supposed to be there so I tried to grab his hand, but there was nothing there.

"But you're dead!" I said.

"Yeah . . .," he admitted a little sheepishly, "but it's no big deal." He smiled and then I knew that he was truly dead, but he was still my friend and it really wasn't anything to worry about. I woke up feeling better and later, when I went out to the truck, I noticed that the little red EGR light on the dash was always lit because the Exhaust Gas Recycling system was disconnected. So that's when I named the truck, patting him affectionately on the dash and saying, "Okay, Edgar, let's go."

It's become a habit now over the years, patting the dash from time to time to urge the old beater on or to thank him for pulling through for me despite my chronic neglect.

I thought about Steve and his permanent solution to his temporary problem while I waited for the bus. Maybe the dead do give us gifts, like the old tales say. I know I needed one that afternoon, even if it was just a matter of having something to compare to my immediate problems.

There was the cluster, for instance, which was scary enough, and now the boy was in trouble at school, suspended for three days for theft. The vice principal had called me just an hour before to tell me that my son and a buddy of his had stolen money from a teacher's purse. He's a bright kid, good-natured and likable, but he's thirteen.

So far this year, five teenage boys have killed themselves in our end of the county, three by gunshot and two by hanging. A sixth boy, thirteen years old and one of my son's buddies, shot himself in the right temple with an antique revolver two weeks ago but will survive with the aid of a glass eye, reconstructive surgery, and counseling. Add him and the other boys to the eleven girls who have also made attempts, and you've got a real problem.

It's called a teenage suicide cluster, and it's an epidemic that can't be diagnosed until it's too late to do much about it. Everyone wonders, "Who's next?" and everyone has a theory: mass hysteria, deteriorating family values, the spotted owl, drugs, domestic violence, too many poor people, satanism, rock 'n' roll, secular humanism.

Four long-distance phone calls get you in touch with a New York City researcher, one of the nation's leading experts. She gives you a straight answer based on years of study and government grants. "We just don't know. We have some theories, but no one really knows why these things happen."

Tuesday afternoon, waiting for the bus. Christmas vacation starts Saturday and I wonder, "Who's next?"

"Shit, Bob," my buddy Jim, over in Prineville, sighed over the phone. "Mass ennui. Just giving up. Wanting to get laid and being afraid of it too, and masturbating; the guilt and the doubt and the hypocrisy of school and all the *shit* you go through—that horrible feeling, sitting in limbo, loneliness and restlessness and 'What's the use?'

"Hell, I remember there were times I thought about snuffing myself, lots of times. You did too, I know you must have—anybody says they didn't think about suicide is a goddamn liar."

"Yeah," I said, "I remember—it's a wonder anyone ever survives."

The bus was late. Or I was early and anxious. It was cold out, and everyone was talking snow. The woodpile was low, and I decided that we'd try to go firewood cutting the next day, before Brushy Butte got snowed in. Put him to work, give him something to do besides sitting around the house all day when he should be in school. Give me something to do besides staring at the flickering cursor on my computer screen.

Edgar's worn-down clutch might blow out on the muddy landing and leave us stranded up there. But even if that happened and we had to hoof it four miles out to the county road, at least we'd be busy instead of just sitting around feeling sorry for ourselves. Besides, we really didn't have enough wood at home to stay warm during even a middling cold snap.

I was trying to figure out what to say to the boy when we had the talk that I knew I would start off by asking, "Well, what happened?" I knew I'd have to be hard on him, but not too hard—not with the cluster going on.

Last summer's star thistle stood dry and gray and popped-corn white along the railroad tracks. I could see the river running steelhead-fishing green through the bare tree branches. The South Umpqua turns that beautiful color when it settles down after a muddy brown winter rise, and I always think of Chalchiutlicue, the Aztec goddess of earthly waters, whose name means "Her Skirt Is Made of Jade."

The bus came over the hump in the road, pulled up at old George's driveway, honked, and backed up into it for the turnaround. The door swung open and Keith Gaynor's little grandson got out, but he was the only one. I looked through my windshield at Betty, the driver, and saw her shrug and pick up a microphone.

"He didn't get on the bus," her amplified voice said, and she shrugged again and pulled out, heading back toward town.

I remember sitting in the Highland Park police station waiting for my dad. I was fourteen then and my buddy Pat Miles and I had been arrested for shoplifting. A store clerk had chased us for three blocks and dragged us back to the store, where we waited for the LAPD to haul us off in handcuffs. It was in June 1966, while my father was recovering from his second heart attack.

I remember how worried he looked when he came into the room and shook hands with the detective. Dad was only forty-six then, but he was gray-haired from raising nine children and worn down by coronary heart disease. On the way home I promised to stay out of trouble with the police. Three months later, just a few days before I started high school, my father died. A few years ago I finally stopped blaming myself for his death, though I still regret having worried him.

I kept my promise for four years before I got arrested again, for vagrancy, in Arizona. My accomplice, Pat, was in and out of juvenile hall and drug rehabilitation programs during those years. He finally hung himself in a jail cell at eighteen years of age.

Where was he? Why didn't he get on the bus and come home? It wasn't supposed to be like this. At least, it never occurred to me that the lumpy-headed little bald guy who once lay in my lap would someday scare the hell out of me.

I followed the bus back to town, wanting to swing Edgar impatiently around the fat yellow rear end of the school bus. Instead, I lit a cigarette and ticked off the half-dozen places he might be, trying to replace my speculative visions with a search plan: check the school first, then the Super Y Market, then downtown to the park, the mini-mart, Stan's Market, the baseball card shop, the Dairy Queen, and then—what? Keep cruising, watch the sidewalks, stop any of his buddies I ran into and ask them if they'd seen him.

There was a basketball game going on in the gym, and I spotted one of the half-wild Steltz boys up in the stands. I made my way past the scorers' table, and he spotted me coming. "Hey, Bob, what's up?" he called down to me.

"Hey, Jerry, hey, you seen my boy?"

"Yeah, he's up at detention. Him and Jesse were late for Mrs. Fent's class."

"Thanks, man. I was wondering why he wasn't on the bus."

"Yeah, he's up there."

"Okay, thanks."

I saw him sitting in a classroom with a half-dozen other boys and girls, all of them staring at the blank blackboard and watching the clock while a teacher sat correcting papers.

Twenty minutes later he came out with the rest of them. "Hi, Dad," he said.

"Hi, son. Detention, huh?"

"Yeah, I was late for class again."

"Well, I wondered why you wasn't on the bus, now I know."

"Yeah," he said, and we walked out to the truck.

He knew and I knew what was coming, but neither of us said anything until I turned onto the old road along the river, toward the dump, instead of crossing the bridge toward home.

"Where're we going?" he asked.

"Out to the rifle range," I told him. "I figured we'd take a walk down by the river."

"I was gonna wait till we got home."

I pulled off the road after a mile and crossed the ruts and puddles in front of the targets, rounded pebbles and shell casings crunching under Edgar's tires. I headed down to the brush line along the river. We got out and walked to the bank, and he sat down on a boulder. I picked up a rock and chucked it into the green water. "Well," I asked, "what happened?"

We were out on a muddy landing up on Brushy Butte the next afternoon, searching through last summer's logging slash for the good dry madrone branches that sound like baseball bats when you chuck them. It started to snow when we had about two thirds of a load, a few light flakes at first and then heavier showers, like gauzy curtains hiding the far side of the draw.

It built up on our hats and shoulders and the roof of the truck while we worked. The saw's chain was getting dull and the slash was turning white, making it hard to pick out the good wood in the tangle of logs and branches. I buzzed up one last chinquapin to top off the load, and we loaded up the saw and maul and water jug, the oil jug and gas can, and jumped into the pickup cab.

I started the engine, and while we waited for it to warm up he asked me one of those questions he likes to ask. "Why does God make snow, Dad? I mean, what's the use of it?"

"Well, it don't run off quick like rain, soaks in good when it melts, so I guess that's one reason. But who knows? It's pretty, and He's an artist after all, so maybe He just likes to see the hills all covered with white."

"Yeah, maybe so. I never thought about that."

Hills and the heads of old people too, it occurred to me. He likes them white. That's why He gives us teenagers—it's a wonder any of us survive. But I kept that notion to myself.

"Well, let's see if we can get out of here without getting stuck in a blizzard."

"Come on, Edgar!" he urged the old truck, patting the dashboard. "You can do it. Go, Edgar, go!"

SNOW

The snow always comes as a surprise, even when you smell it coming, and the weatherman tells you it's coming, and everyone in the valley is talking about the snow coming, and you see the sleet splattering on your windshield at sunset. Somehow you're never prepared for the reality of snow.

It comes so quietly in the night, in soggy clumps at first and then as tiny drifting flakes, each whirling crystal unlike any other that ever was or will be again. Snowflakes have the carefree innocence of all things brief and beautiful, which fills us with sadness because they remind us of our own short stay here.

Of course, it's only us who feel that way. Watching the snowflakes fall, it's hard to imagine them carrying anything but joy in their whirling hearts. They are born in the bellies of clouds, tiny specks of earth's dust that clothe themselves in glittering sea moisture like debutantes dressing up in lace and jewels for a waltz on the winds. Believe me, though they never speak, they have their own soft song as they dance, singly or holding hands in the sky, before they settle on the valley.

Even though we mutter about inconvenience as we make our way to the woodpile, or sit listening to icy road reports and school closures over a cup of coffee in the morning, our first and deepest reaction is delight. Like children bursting forth from the house to play, our hearts jump at the sight of the world transformed.

How strange it is to look out of windows edged in feathery crystal patterns of frost, to see sunlight split into rainbows by the icicle prisms dangling from the roof's eaves, to look out on fields of unbroken white snow.

The leafless fruit trees, oaks, and maples, so stark in winter rains, reveal their delicate tracery when clothed in snow. Fence rails and posts, so common that they're almost invisible, stand out suddenly when piled high with white powder. How green and vulnerable the small patches of grass look, in sheltered nooks surrounded by the frozen snow. How warm and cozy it seems inside by the wood stove.

FUJI AND THE WAR

ON YOUNG MEN

Fuji wanted to know what I did. "You are student?" he asked.

We were standing beside Interstate 40 in Albuquerque in the spring of 1970. I wasn't a student anymore. Two months earlier I had dropped out of high school. There was a war going on in those days, and I was living on a commune founded by the Up Against the Wall Motherfuckers. But how do you explain that to a young Japanese hitchhiker who barely speaks English?

"No, I live in a commune," I told him, pointing at the Sandia mountains, whose broken, jagged strata rose in the distance. "It's a farm, you know. I'm a farmer."

"Fah mah?"

"Yeah, you know, a farmer. Make things grow?"

He brought out a multilingual dictionary with a red plastic cover. I searched through seven different languages, but there was no translation of the word in any of them.

I looked up from the book. The young man grinned brightly back. He looked like some All-American teenager out of an Archie comic. I wondered what he thought, how he saw America, here on a freeway on-ramp in the timeless pastel landscape of the West. How could I explain my own arrival here a few minutes earlier, with thirty-eight cents in my pocket and an eight-hundred-mile journey to Los Angeles ahead? What's the Japanese word for hippie?

"You are not student?" he asked.

"No, I'm a . . ." A what? It's hard enough to label yourself in the best of times. Most people give their occupational title, but I didn't have a job and I had a deep distrust of labels. Like Alice, I knew who I used to be, but I'd been through several changes since then. "A farmer. We grow food, you know, corn and beans and stuff."

He was clearly puzzled. "You go to university?"

Only to panhandle or to score. What could I tell him that would be both true and understandable? Truth was everything. Whatever it was it had to be devoid of pretense. A would-be saint? An acidhead? A poet? An outlaw? There was truth enough in all of these. But I saw myself as a gentleman farmer, someone who cultivated plants and whose desire was simply to be left alone and to let the world go to hell on its own.

There was a lull in the traffic. I squatted down and pantomimed the act of planting a seed, choosing a piece of gravel and carefully burying and watering it. I made chopping motions with an invisible hoe. My hands traced the growth of the seed into a plant and then the harvesting and eating. I looked up eagerly, hoping to see the light of understanding in his face. He had a deeply puzzled and vaguely embarrassed look on his face.

"Shit. You don't understand?"

"No. You are student?"

"Yeah . . . I'm a student."

"I am student too. I go to university in Japan."

A state police patrol car cruised by, and I tightened reflexively. It didn't stop though. New Mexico cops were relatively easy to deal with anyway, not like in L.A., where a cop would, as often as not, approach me with a drawn pistol just to run a computer ID check. I don't think that New Mexico even had a police computer system in those days.

It was a sort of game—Blue Meanies versus the Flower Children—though the consequences were quite serious. We accepted our roles, after all. There was a war going on, and this was the America of Richard J. Daley and Abbie Hoffman. You could tell by looking at the uniform which side someone was on. Everyone knew, except for Fuji.

Fuji didn't notice the cops. He stood, arm uplifted in an exaggerated hitchhiker pose, like a stick figure beside the highway, while a small school of cars streamed past and we failed to hook one.

It's easy to feel insignificant when standing beside an interstate trying to catch a ride. The cars and trucks pass by in chromed and enameled self-sufficiency, and as the hours go by you feel yourself blending in with the rest of the landscape, becoming a weathered roadside fixture. You can fight it for a while, read the scrawled messages on traffic signs, toss pebbles, scratch out designs in the dirt. Eventually, you lose your sense of self-proportion; half-conscious, you swell to mountain size and shrink to mouse dimensions. Finally, you draw numbed indifference about yourself like a cloak.

But hitchhiking with Fuji made the world all new. I saw with his eyes the strangeness of the familiar desert, felt the intensity of blue sky, wondered at the distant convoluted mountains, smelled the cleansing sagebrush. Even the wide gray bands of pavement reaching for infinity seemed charged with meaning.

"It is very beautiful," he said. "America is very beautiful." I agreed.

Beauty abounded, everywhere, if you had the eyes to see it. It could be seen in the smallest of things, a scrap of weathered wood, an old shoe. In quiet moments, the powerful simplicity of things, the subtle nobility inherent in them would reach me. At times I could see it in everything and everyone, no matter what the scale, an essential something that eluded definition but that could be experienced as beauty. It had become, for me, the proofmark of reality and the basis for my morality.

Fuji too, it seemed, understood the importance of beauty. We would travel together then, sharing the journey, tasting the sweetness of the ancient landscape of the Southwest, exulting in mountains and mesas and limitless sky. That one word, "beautiful," was all the language we would need.

Just before we caught our first ride, a jet flew overhead, to Fuji's delight.

"F-104, very good plane!" he beamed. He told me that he lived near an American air force base back home in Japan, and he rattled off the names of various aircraft frequenting the place. "U.S. Air Force number 1! Very good planes."

His enthusiasm for military technology set me back. Didn't he know there was a war going on? I'd made my own decision a month before by not registering for the draft, a crime punishable by five years in prison. I feared prison but expected to end up there eventually, since every encounter with the police was a potential arrest for violating the Selective Service laws.

How could my companion praise the machinery of death and destruction? Had he forgotten our fathers' war? How could he? I grew up killing Japs with toy guns and avocado hand grenades.

Still, his enthusiasm had been genuine and innocent. He had meant his praise as a compliment of sorts, a tribute to my country's ability to build fast, sophisticated planes. He must not have known that he was traveling through a nation in which the issue of peace had divided us into armed camps. He couldn't have known that the war in Asia had its counterpart here at home or that the twin wars were really just two equally ugly fronts in one war, the war on young men.

I have heard that the death rate for American men ages eighteen to twenty-five was higher in the late sixties than it was during World War II. I can believe it. In those days, if the Viet Cong or the cops didn't get you, life on the streets, drugs, random violence, suicide, or car accidents could.

Two weeks earlier, on this same highway, a trucker had tried to run me over, steering his double-trailer semi ten feet onto the road shoulder to the spot where I'd stood moments before. It had happened at dusk when the highway was empty. Later that summer, outside of Denver, a beer bottle tossed from a passing car exploded against a traffic sign three feet behind me and about a foot over my head. On a freeway on-ramp in San Bernardino a middle-aged man driving a bobtail truck gave me the finger, his face contorted in a mask of sheer hatred. Wherever I went that summer, from Oregon to Florida, one message was made clear: my kind weren't wanted.

It has been over twenty years now since that spring, and it was one of many road trips I made hitchhiking all over America, as bereft of money as I was of purpose. It must have taken us several rides from start to finish, but I can only recall the first and last of them.

A battered beige Ford station wagon pulled over for us, and we grabbed our packs and ran up the roadside without discussing war and peace. The driver was a fat middle-aged Chicano, and a Navajo woman was sitting in the passenger seat. He was a social worker giving her a ride to Gallup. The woman spoke Navajo and Spanish but no English. The driver spoke English, Spanish, and Navajo. He was delighted to have a Japanese student on board and kept asking him how to say different phrases in Japanese. He tuned in to the Navajo radio station, but Fuji didn't understand a word of it, although Navajo sounds a lot like Japanese to me.

At a roadside rest area on the way to Gallup, I asked Fuji where he would be staying when we got to L.A. He didn't have anyplace to stay there, so I told him he could flop with me at a friend's house once we hit town.

He accepted and thanked me. "You have beautiful heart," he told me. There's no higher compliment.

The last ride came just before dark, in that time when colors lose their value and the world is seen in silhouette. We were standing in front of an abandoned gas station on the outskirts of Holbrook or maybe Winslow, Arizona, when a semi pulled over for us, and we clambered up into the high cab with the driver.

Fuji crawled into the sleeper behind the seats, and I sat in the passenger seat. The driver was tired and needed somebody to talk to so he could stay awake. I was approaching exhaustion myself, but since Fuji couldn't speak enough English to keep the conversation going, I sat up with the driver while my partner slept and we bounced through the night.

The trucker said that he was heading to San Bernardino and would be arriving there around sunup, providing we both stayed awake. The truck wasn't a very comfortable ride, but it beat sleeping with the scorpions and rattlesnakes by the roadside.

We climbed the long grade up to Flagstaff, the trucker constantly shifting his gears and adjusting his lights with toggle switches on the dashboard. It was my first ride in a semi, and I felt like I'd made the grade as an official hitchhiker.

Between Williams and Kingman the truck developed an ominous clunking, something wrong in the drive train somewhere. The driver pulled over and looked around beneath the truck with a flashlight. It was a moonless, starry night, and the headlights cast long shadows that were swallowed up in the darkened desert.

Fuji sat up in the sleeper space and rubbed his eyes. He'd slept through the bumping and clunking of the truck, but the stillness awakened him. "We are in California?" he asked.

"No, Arizona. The truck's broke down."

"Broke down?"

"Yeah, it's broken. It don't work."

"Ah, broken. We walk?"

"Maybe. I don't know, we'll see."

We sat in the uncertain glow of the cab's dashlights, our ride a mote in the dark as lone as any star. Hunger and exhaustion were catching up with me. My mind filled the blackness with bright speckled patterns moving in drunken waltz time.

The driver returned from his inspection. "Damn U-joint's going out. We'll wing it into Kingman. I'll call in and see if the company wants to have it fixed there or if we can try and make it to San Berdoo."

"We stay," I told my road partner. There was more I wanted to tell him, about the odds of getting arrested in Kingman. I'd heard all about Kingman. I should have warned Fuji, but there was the language barrier and, more importantly, there was too much to explain that wouldn't make sense to him, a traveler in a country whose problems he didn't understand.

"Well, I hope we keep going," I told the driver.

"Oh well, ain't nothing we can do now. It's up to the dispatcher. If he tells me to 'park 'er,' I gotta park 'er."

It was a long, slow ride in the heaving semi into Kingman. Fuji went back to sleep, and the driver and I didn't talk much, both of us busy with our own worries.

Kingman was a strip town, a string of neon signs three or four miles long. The driver pulled into a graveled lot next to a corrugated metal repair shop and

....

made a phone call from a pay booth. Fuji woke up and I explained to him that we might go on with the truck or we might have to walk out of town.

The truck stayed; we walked. We walked less than a half-mile, our backpacks patting us reassuringly, before a squad car pulled up alongside us with the blue lights flashing. A big blond cop with an American flag patch on his sleeve got out to question us. He checked our ID, amused by Fuji's passport with its seals and incomprehensible writing, and suspicious about my lack of a draft card. I told him I'd lost it and was on my way to L.A. to get a new one.

"I bet you burned it," he replied. "Well, you're coming with me." Then he turned to Fuji. "You can go." He brought out his handcuffs and locked my wrists together behind my back.

It took Fuji a moment to realize what was happening. Confusion gave way to dismay on his face, and he tried to ask why I was being arrested.

"My friend, he . . ."

"You go," the cop told him. "He's coming with me."

"I'm sorry, man, I got to go." I told him. "It's okay." What could I say? I was sure that I was on my way to five years in prison. I worried, though, that he would think he'd been traveling with an escaped convict.

"Go on. Get out of here. He's going to jail. You go," the cop said over his shoulder as he hustled me into the back seat. I turned to look at Fuji as the cop closed the

....

door. He was standing there looking shocked and confused, sad and lonely.

"Goodbye," I said, feeling sorrier for him than I did for myself. He still didn't believe what was happening, I could see that in his eyes. He came over to the window and he wanted to say something, but the words weren't there.

"I'm sorry," I said. "Really. Goodbye."

DEGREES OF UNDERSTANDING

It's always encouraging to hear from someone who admires your work. After all, freelance writing is a remarkably unrewarding career, a lonely and distant business where you send pieces off into the world like orphan babies to be adopted by utter strangers. You wonder what sort of homes they'll find, whether the children you bore through weeks or months of careful labor will be loved and cared for or neglected and abused.

You tuck them into a manila envelope pinned with a note that pleads for a chance to have a good home, and then you worry about their reception. Will they live on to support you and survive you and perhaps to help give birth to future generations? Or will they die prematurely, lying at the bottom of a cockatiel cage thousands of miles away? You drop them into the dark void of a Postal Service mailbox, and all you can do is hope they have the strength to walk on their own.

I recently received a phone call from a local journalist who had read one of my essays in a literary magazine. She seemed quite excited by it, which was flattering of course, and I thanked her for her kind words.

I wallowed in the reporter's praise like a grinning dog rolling on a summer lawn as she described her chance encounter with my work in a Portland bookstore. She'd been struck by the insights my piece had given her. Out of curiosity, she had checked the biographical notes in the back and was amazed to find that we lived in the same small rural community.

She asked me a few questions about the essay and about my career, which I answered easily, but then she asked a tough one: "Is it true that you're a high school dropout?"

The question is always a little hard for me to deal with. Usually, the topic comes up less directly when I'm asked, "So, where did you go to school?" It's one that used to embarrass me. Somehow, I guess, which college you've attended is supposed to be a measure of something—but I'm not sure just what.

"I'm a high school dropout," I usually tell them. Strictly speaking, that's not the truth, though it's close enough for strangers. Besides, the truth is a bit complicated and it's a line that gets a satisfying reaction, so why not fudge a bit?

Actually, Eagle Rock High School and I gave up on each other. "Fail to honor people and they fail to honor you," as Lao-tzu says. We were caught up in a game of mutual disrespect—the beginnings of the game were lost, but it ended when I loaded up a backpack and hitchhiked around the country for several months.

I was supposed to do well in school. My Scholastic Aptitude Test scores always ranked me in the top one percent. And yet I had a tremendous antipathy toward schooling—perhaps a Scholastic Attitude Test would have been more useful.

Two conflicting views of why anyone would bother to learn were presented to me as a student. The first was that learning was a noble and joyful thing, worthy of pursuit for its own sake. The other was that poor grades spelled financial ruin. "If you don't do well in school, you'll never get a decent job," was the refrain. I could feel the truth of the first proposition because I enjoyed learning things regardless of their utility. But the second proposition smacked of coercion, and I could never understand what grades had to do with the acquisition of knowledge.

There was something inherently false about schooling, which I sensed but could not articulate. I saw it in the faces of students cramming for final exams and in the faces of teachers who wished they were elsewhere.

Learning has turned out to be a lifelong joy, and I never have managed to find a decent job, so I guess both propositions contained equal truth. I spent my first ten years out of school working thirty different jobs as a laborer.

After an on-the-job accident left me partially disabled, I found myself unable to labor full time and so I taught myself to write, a job with more prestige but considerably less income than laboring. I fell (ten feet, headfirst) into it. A ladder twisted out from under me and, like Alice down the rabbit hole, I was pitched into a bewildering world of chronic pain and humiliation—the worker's compensation system.

For the first time in my life, I was unable to work. After years of defining yourself through pride in your body's strength and endurance, it is hard to find yourself disabled. Poems are written about athletes whose careers are cut tragically short by injury or death, but a laborer who gets crunched on the job is merely categorized as a "flake" and discarded.

I was told to get work pumping gasoline, but I turned to my typewriter for solace and challenge instead. It was a new world to compete in, but I felt sure that hard work and stubborn persistence would eventually pay off in my literary labors as they had in the woods and mills and construction sites. (Like so many notions in my life, this one turned out to be correct but terribly naive.) Most of what I earn still comes from hiring myself out for the odd jobs that come my way.

Although I earned my General Education Diploma and even completed a freshman writing class at a community college, most of my notions about higher education come from dealing with college students and graduates. It's not fashionable to speak of class differences here in America, where we cherish the belief that we live in a classless society. Yet I admit that I am aware of the differences between myself and the academically educated.

My background has given me an understandable, perhaps unavoidable, belief that blue-collar workers are generally better people than white-collar workers and professionals. There's an element of sour grapes in that, to be sure, but truly, I do believe that working indoors stunts human beings just as a lack of sunlight stunts plants.

It's hard for me to trust people who haven't worked in the woods and the fields, in the mills and on construction sites. It's hard for me to trust people who have a college education and the prejudices that go with it— not that I am without prejudices myself, but mine are simply different. Even highly educated, sensitive, liberal people suffer from prejudices that are difficult to overcome because they are so deeply ingrained.

I remember arguing with an editor once, a very refined woman, telling her that artistic sensibility was an inherent trait that crossed class lines. "Just because you're a poet or a dancer or a sculptor, that doesn't mean that you appreciate beauty any more than a logger or a field hand does," I told her, thinking about an old gyppo logger I knew. "Nonsense," she said, "of course it does."

I wondered at her ignorance and concluded that she couldn't see in others what she had never looked for in them. Elitism is a sign of ignorance, an ignorance that is the result of the blinding effects of prejudice—refined and cultured prejudice certainly, but prejudice nonetheless.

There is an outlook that laborers develop that is hard to explain to people who haven't done manual labor. It comes from a life of pain, pride, and desperation, from having to prove over and over again that you can keep up with anyone, and knowing that someday you won't be able to outwork the others.

We trust what we know. My knowledge is from the perceptions of my body rather than my mind. I can't believe in abstractions, the world of ideas, theories, propositions, and labels, where what something is called is more important than what it actually is. The world of mind seems dwarfed and dull to me when compared to the opulence of physical reality.

This physical education, the lessons that I carry in my body, my mind, and my psyche, is difficult to express and perhaps impossible to teach using words. What I've learned may not be the sort of things that lessons are made of (at least the kind of lessons that can be embodied in an essay). What do you learn from fifty-hour weeks of pulling and stacking lumber except tolerance to noise, fatigue, and pain?

Having worked for a number of college grads over the years, I found them to be oddly incompetent and overly self-conscious. They seemed to be full of technical expertise yet utterly unfit for handling laborers. It was as if they'd learned to substitute facts for fortitude and tentative answers for tenacious actions.

I'm not ashamed of having earned five college credits and a 4.0 GPA. I learned some useful things in my brief time there, but I'm more proud of my years at Sidewalk University's School of Hard Knocks, where I earned a B.A. (Busting Ass) degree and an M.S. (More of the Same).

A friend of mine, who dropped out of the same high school at the same time as I did, used to work as a mechanic. A few years ago he had his own garage in the small town where we both live. One day he was in the shop working on a pickup truck and had his tape player cranked up, listening to music while he worked. He looked up from the engine to see a well-dressed man standing in the open doorway with a puzzled expression on his face.

"He was staring at me like I was a two-headed monkey," my friend told me. "So I went over and said 'Hi! Can I help you?' The guy says, 'I was just passing by and, uh, well . . . That's . . . that's J. S. Bach!' like he couldn't believe it, you know. So I said, 'Yeah, it's the Cologne Symphony doing the *Third Brandenburg*. Heck of a nice recording, ain't it?' And he just stood there like he couldn't figure it out, you know, 'What the hell's going on here?' The poor dude, it just blew his mind, I guess. I felt like I ought to put on some Merle Haggard just to make him feel at ease."

My friend was right to feel pity for his visitor. After all, nothing in the man's education had prepared him for this. Apparently no one had ever told him that formal education can't create a love of great art or that a lack of formal education won't stop people from admiring it.

He'd learned instead a set of prejudices concerning the value of institutionalized education. He'd been led to believe that somehow the money he was spending and the time he was investing in academic studies were going to buy him a place among an elite group whose refined taste was their exclusive property.

Academics have an undeniable economic interest in promoting this brand of prejudice. Of course, this pecuniary interest is never a direct cause—that is really taking the charge too far—but it's undoubtedly an unconscious factor that hinders any questioning of the underlying assumptions.

I have another friend who earned a master's degree in creative writing and has never sold a piece to a paying market. He teaches English and uses some of my essays as models of good writing for his students to study. He finds it ironic, as I do, that over the many years of our friendship, he's made more money talking about those essays than I did by writing them, and that he earns a living as a certified master of a craft in which he has never done journeyman-level work.

A university degree is not a reliable measure of sensitivity, talent, competence, knowledge, or wisdom. It is, however, a sort of password among those who decide who to hire and who not to hire for certain positions. It says, "I am one of you. I share your outlook. I know how to play by the same rules you play by." Of course, the mechanic's overalls, the logger's suspenders and hickory shirt, and the trucker's baseball cap say the same thing and serve the same purpose. Ignorance and prejudice are not the exclusive property of any class, but then neither are sensitivity, talent, competence, knowledge, and wisdom.

PAINTING A HOUSE

Well-diggers lead the water wherever they like;
fletchers shape the arrow; carpenters bend a log of
wood; wise people fashion themselves.

⌒ The Sutta Pitaka
circa 250 B.C.

I was taught house painting
by a friend who'd learned the trade from two old men. As
he instructed me in the rudiments of the craft, I could
hear their voices and attitudes coming through him to
me, an old-fashioned way of working that conjured up
visions of medieval artisans raising cathedrals, because
along with the mundane matters of scraping and sanding,
there was an insistence on propriety.

Each instruction was accompanied by the phrase
"the professional painter . . ."—a standard that drew me
irresistibly to emulation, like "the superior man" of Lao-
tzu. In every facet of the work, from cleaning the

buckets to holding the brush, I found that there were many ways to do it but only one way acceptable to a real professional.

Gradually, I learned to discern the difference between a well-done job and an unskilled or careless one. Driving by a painting crew on the way to work, my friend would assess their level of professionalism in a matter of minutes, by the way the painters were dressed, the manner of their preparations, the layout of their tools, the number, positioning, and quality of their tarps, or the brand of paint they used. I found that the difference between a properly done job and shoddy work lay in the amount of attention paid to uncountable minute details, any one of which would seem inconsequential in itself.

Like life itself, a building being painted offers an almost endless series of decisions. Anyone can quickly color a house with new paint, but how well it will stand up over time depends on the work you can't see, the care taken to prepare it before the paint goes on.

Every house has a painted record of the care and abuse that has been given it over the years. A good house painter can read it as easily as you would a comic book. The scars of use and the marks of time wear away at the paint, of course, and demand attention. But much of the work is concerned with the efforts of past painters, finding and correcting sins of omission: careless sanding, drips, overspray, thin spots and unpainted surfaces tucked away in obscure nooks, cheap paint—all the little "fuck it" spots where somebody, either through lack of effort or skill, didn't take the time to do it right.

~~~

House painting, like any craft, changes its practitioners. Somehow the rhythms of the work and the habits it requires alter the painter. It's a slow process, much like the work itself, a lot of minor, step-by-step changes, seemingly endless when you're in the busy-doing middle of things, that can only be appreciated afterwards.

Breaking a huge task down into a series of necessary steps teaches patience and hope—good training for attempting any lengthy labor, whether social reform, writing a novel, or having a fruitful marriage. Anything worth doing takes time, discipline, and attention to details. "The professional painter," my friend told me, "is never in a hurry."

There is a steadiness that results from the discipline of repeating an orderly process. It begins on the physical level and slowly shapes the mind and spirit as well. The work transforms the worker, inevitably. Conscientiously done work makes us conscious, while careless work makes unfeeling zombies of us. It also shapes our world, making it tidy or sloppy, beautiful or ugly, according to our attitude in the making of it.

~~~

A few years ago, while I was painting a big old rambling, two-story house, I found myself ready to die. I was finishing up the month-long job, painting the trim on an attic dormer that sat too far back from the edge to be reached with the long aluminum ladder. It was dangerous, but no more dangerous than a lot of things I've done over the years working on houses, and I was being careful. As I carried my brush and paint bucket across the steep roof, I realized clearly that I might die trying to paint that house. It was an odd feeling, not a suicidal or ominous one—I just felt that I was ready.

The thought didn't hold any terror or grief for me, and I found that I didn't have any regrets. I was simply ready to accept death. It was a very contented feeling really. Death didn't seem so bad after all and neither did life.

It lent a kind of grace to my work. Everything I did while filled with the acceptance of my own death took on a stateliness, like a calming ceremony. Somehow the work, the day, and my self were stripped of pretension and clearly just were, without encumbrances.

As with most manual labor, painting involves a lot of time doing work that doesn't require much mental concentration. Chipping, scraping, sanding, and washing walls keeps the hands busy and leaves time for reflection. Adolf Hitler painted houses for a living, and I can easily imagine him in spattered white overalls, mulling over the social problems of his time up on a ladder, just as Eric

Hoffer pondered the nature of fanaticism while loading and unloading ships in San Francisco.

Of course, the work of preparing a house to be painted isn't really mindless at all, but in the early stages it is the choices that require attention more than the work itself. Later, as the coats of paint build up, there's a reversal. The choices become fewer, and the execution becomes more demanding.

It is the final work, painting the trim, that demands the most careful concentration in the doing and the least thought as to how to do it. The order is invariable, governed by a few simple rules: work the edges before the middle, the top before the bottom, the inside before the outside. What should be done is easily stated, but how it's done will make or break the job.

Every painter keeps a special brush, called a sash tool, for painting window frames, door panels, and the fine details. A good painter babies this brush, cleaning it with great care and storing it lovingly after use. These brushes vary in size and shape and materials, angle-cut or straight-cut, ox tail or boar bristle, and each painter will pick one type and use no other.

It's a wonderful, sensual feeling, laying the paint on, like petting a cat. To get the paint to lie just right takes a steady hand, a good eye, and a physical attentiveness that keeps the mind from wandering; you concentrate only on the flow of bristles across the wood. The long, even strokes that pull the paint to the edge without touching the glass must not waver. Too close, they spread over onto the glass; too far, and the edge looks ragged with bits of the old paint showing.

Your body responds to the rhythms of the work, breathing in time to the long strokes that spread the paint evenly and, despite the slowness of movement, more quickly than short ones.

Body and mind and the work act on each other and shape and limit each other in complex ways. It's difficult to say just how and why, and every job is a special case, but in the end there's a result, an undeniable record of all that went into it.

⁂

I once took on a job painting a radiator shop as part of a barter deal. Lonesome Pickup Bert, my geriatric 1948 Chevy, needed an expensive new radiator, and the old metal building needed painting.

Decades of paint hung in great peeling, multicolored flakes from the place, giving it the sad look of a molting chicken. The landlord, I learned, was an old-world craftsman called Herman the German, a man whose drive toward perfection had led him to spend seventeen years in the construction of a commercial building across the street. Herman's work had been studied and documented by a host of building inspectors, architects, engineers, and professors who came to marvel over the workmanship of the place.

I thought of Herman the German constantly as we scraped and sandblasted. It was one of the oldest metal buildings of its kind in Los Angeles, one of the first gas stations in town, an ornate steel box full of odd angles, exposed nuts and bolts, tiny glass panes, and decorative trim, built just before America's entrance into the First World War.

I was determined to make the tattered old bird rise like a bright phoenix from the ashes of neglect, but I grew more and more dissatisfied as the enormity of the task unfolded itself in the work. As the expenses of time and money mounted, I found myself forced to compromise on my goal of perfection.

Near the end of the job, I was up on a ladder painting the thin iron window frames when I heard a thickly accented voice speaking to me from below.

"You boys are doing a very good chob," he said.

I turned to see an old man smiling up from below. The ancient master craftsman had finally stopped by to look at his rental. "Well," I offered lamely, "it could be better."

"Better?" laughed the old man. "*Ja, ja,* it *could* be better—*always,* it could be better. But you are doing a good chob. It is enough."

I was delighted by the praise, of course, and only later did I realize that he'd revealed a secret: not perfect but good. Craftsmanship is a matter of compromise because imperfection is the nature of reality. "The professional painter," like "the superior man," knows this.

We paint our lives like this too, close—as close to perfection as the exigencies of time and material and energy allow—but never perfectly. To strive for perfection and to accept falling short gracefully is the way of sanity.

Knowing that achieving perfection is impossible brings humor and compassion into our lives by allowing us to take comfort in satisfaction. Living a life is a type of work too, and it comes to an end as every job does, and the result can only be judged by the effort and skill that went into it.

COUNTING HEADS

The first thing I had to do was to abandon the speech we'd rehearsed, which, if I recall correctly, began with something like: "Hello, my name is (your name). I am an enumerator with the United States Department of Commerce (display your badge) and we are conducting the 1990 census in your neighborhood. With your permission, I would like to ask you a few questions regarding your household."

No one talks like that around here, and it would be profoundly rude to adopt such a tone with my neighbors. Instead, the typical conversation began something like this:

"Mornin', ma'am. How you doin'?"

"Why, just fine, thank you. How 'bout yourself?"

"Oh, pretty fair—can't complain. Looks like we're in for another hot one, but I reckon it beats bein' out in the rain, anyway."

"Yeah, I s'pose it does. You the census man?"

"Yes, ma'am. I hate to bother you like this, but you know how the government is, it's gotta get done. You got a minute?"

The government's notion was to be productive and professional, that is, impersonal. But you just can't ask people for personal information and walk out on them without leaving a little something in return. It didn't have to be much, maybe just an acknowledgment that my temporary employer would probably hand out the details of their personal lives to anyone who cared to take a look—if it didn't get lost first. More often, I simply needed to listen to their problems and share a few of my own.

All of this was time-consuming, of course, and for a while I worried about spending too much time sipping coffee at kitchen tables. However, we had been instructed to "follow the local customs," and chewing the fat with the neighbors was demonstrably an integral part of our traditional local culture. Besides, I wouldn't have taken on the task of visiting seven hundred households if it hadn't been for the chance to hear people talk.

When I heard that the job was coming up, I knew immediately I wanted to apply for it. It was an instinctive response, which I later rationalized by deciding that meeting all my neighbors would be good for me as a writer. This was a reasonable and entirely justifiable excuse, but in the end, only an excuse.

The truth is that I, and every writer I've ever met, was a snoop long before taking up "my craft or sullen art." I've always loved eavesdropping on the conversations of strangers, watching their actions with a sidelong glance, secretly delighting in unguarded revelations.

Sometimes the craft is just an excuse for the habit, giving me the sort of professional immunity granted to priests and psychotherapists and census takers. At my more honest times, I see that we writers are really a pitifully maladjusted bunch, hiding behind white sheets of paper, speaking with the great voice to hundreds of thousands of distant people we never meet while keeping our thoughts to ourselves among our neighbors.

The high point, topographically speaking, of my six weeks as an enumerator came when I stood on the bald top of Sheep Hill, the mountain at the foot of which our little shack by the tracks sits. I'd been meaning to climb it for twelve years, but never got more than a third of the way up. Armed with the plastic badge of mandatory cooperation pinned to my shirt, I obtained the key to a locked gate from the telephone company and drove to the summit on a gravel road.

Typically, in this country of jumbled terrain, I had to drive ten miles to reach a point about a mile from my front door—for those with raven wings. It might as well have been Tierra del Fuego or Fargo. To hike it would

....

probably require a tough six hours, round trip, because half of that mile-long "shortest distance between two points" is up.

My official purpose was served the moment I reached the end of the road, just short of the microwave transmission tower. I could say with certainty that no one lived up there without ever leaving the car. But I couldn't turn away without spending a federally funded idle hour enjoying the kind of vista that once served vision quests and is now reserved for utility workers.

Standing on a mountaintop changes your perspective, not just optically but, more importantly, emotionally. The few square miles of valley nestled between ridge tops that make up my day-to-day world seemed both grander and more fragile than I'd imagined. It was as if I stood in two places at once, up above and down below, both laughing Gulliver and self-important Lilliputian.

Gathering information has hazards more dangerous than walking up to a neighbor's porch past ill-tempered dogs. Perhaps the greatest danger was in seeing the data but not the people. For one thing, none of the really important questions appeared on the survey forms. I began to doubt the validity of a statistical abstract in forming a portrait of my community. In the real world, the answer is always the same because, in the end, there's only one of each.

....

As I went from door to door, methodically circling clockwise and always working the homes to my right, I began to toy with the notion of a meaningful survey, devoid of names, gender, age, and occupation but full of the really big questions and with room for answers that might require volumes just to record a single reply.

At every sixth home I conducted an in-depth interview, using a long questionnaire requiring highly personal information about income, jobs, level of education, military service, and health. I was often struck by the contrast between one long-form interview and the next. One elderly couple, living in an old wooden house on a $6,000 pension, reported ten years' worth of elementary school education between the husband and wife. Six houses down the road, a couple in their late twenties were earning over $100,000 annually. Twelve homes up the road, a farmer with a college degree reported working more than sixty hours per week during the previous year for a net loss of $40,000.

On the same mile of road, I met a bartender who lived in a trailer, husbandless and raising two children. She was in a hurry and asked me to come by her establishment that evening. It was a slow night at the bar, with a half-dozen regular customers lined up on the bar stools. I ordered a cup of coffee, and we squeezed the interview in between her duties. One besotted old harpy, sitting three seats down, kept offering advice to the young woman, repeating the same defiant mantra with each question, "Name, address, and Social Security number, honey—that's all you gotta give 'em."

Actually, none of the forms asked for anyone's Social Security number, but the long form did require me to ask for her job title and then a description of her main tasks and duties.

"Mixing and serving drinks," I suggested and began to pencil in my own reply, anticipating her agreement.

"Nope—babysitting drunks," she informed me in all seriousness. I turned my pencil upside down to erase what I'd written and recorded her reply.

Even in its smaller elements (in this case Douglas County voting precinct 63A), a society resembles an untidy rummage sale where cultural artifacts, ranging from cobwebby attitudes left over from days of obsidian tools to this morning's radio talk show topic, crowd together on the same cluttered table. One old farmer, who managed to withhold every bit of information without ever refusing to answer a single question, gave me a rambling account of his family's struggle against government perfidy going back to the days of the Greenback-Labor Party and William Jennings Bryan's Cross of Gold speech.

The joy of discovering traces of the past was one of the first of many unexpected delights I found, and it nearly became an obstacle to the others. To see what is actually there to be seen is harder than digging up stumps.

Our perceptions are so deeply rooted in what we expect to see that we almost never notice what is truly there.

I was determined to understand my neighbors, not just to stockpile ore for the stamping mill of my craft, but out of a sense of social and spiritual duty as well. We are, as members of our society, required to know our community in order to make the informed decisions that, as citizens, we must make. Knowing the issues and ourselves is not enough; we have to know each other as well.

Coupled with the biblical mandate that we love our neighbors, the obligation to know the people we live among becomes an essential matter. It's not merely an ideal goal to work toward; in the most fundamental sense, it is an inescapable necessity. Even from the most pragmatic point of view, we simply can't live an enjoyable life unless we know and, through knowing, love each other.

Looking back on my stint as an information gatherer, the strongest impression I have is of the nearly universal decency of my neighbors. Although many people took the opportunity to complain about the government, and a few refused to cooperate, they were polite about it. Well, almost all of them were polite.

At an isolated trailer house a nervous young couple answered the door and explained that they were just visiting and that their friend had only recently moved into the place. In accordance with my instructions to base the survey on residency as of April 1, 1990, I asked them if they knew the exact date. Before they could reply, a loud male voice began booming, "Wrong! Wrong! Wrong!" from somewhere inside. They looked at each other and then at me in alarm. Then the chanting gave way to a stream of expletives, the drift of which sent me scurrying to my car.

I paused a moment in the car to note the address and check off the appropriate box on the census form before leaving. A bearded, shirtless, skeletal fellow with yellowed, scabrous skin appeared in the doorway and accused me of writing down the license plate number of a van parked in the driveway. A clinical diagnostic term, "amphetamine psychosis," and the possibility of gunfire occurred to me simultaneously.

"You got a problem?" the gaunt man demanded to know. I did, but I took care of it by starting my engine and jamming the transmission into reverse.

Still, no one barked at me other than a speed freak, a barfly, and a few toothsome dogs, and, even then, I never got bitten.

After a few weeks, the wearing effects of concentrated attention finally caught up with me. The sheer number of people and places and conversations I experienced day after day got to be more than I could keep track of. It was then that I became aware of something

I'd felt before but never really fully appreciated—the benefit of being burned out.

When the tide of statistical information and personal observation reached flood stage, it was sink or swim, so I floated instead. I didn't choose to adopt a different attitude. I was simply too overwhelmed to do anything but enjoy what I was doing without adding any layers of moral or intellectual involvement. Oddly, giving up the attempt at understanding allowed me to know more than I'd thought possible.

There are times in each of our lives when for one reason or another we simply can't spare the energy it takes to prop up our self-image. Sometimes this is a very frightening condition, but on other occasions it is a source of great joy. Either way, it is always a time when we are able to learn unexpected things because we're too tired to do anything but directly experience unadulterated reality.

With my attempt to note all the differences among my neighbors a hopeless mess, I finally began to appreciate their underlying sameness. In an unexpected way, by looking for the little things that set my neighbors apart from each other, I'd been ignoring a large part of who they were.

Observations, especially when it comes to people, always tell us more about the observer than the observed. Every conversation is a Rorschach test. Until you have the knack of losing focus or, more properly, of

abandoning your perspective, it's impossible to appreciate the multiplicity of an ordinary human being. When
you simply accept people without attempting to define
them, you learn more about them, even in the briefest
of encounters. With people, face value is full value.

A friend of mine who holds a doctorate in
sociology shuddered when I pointed out to him that
categories of people don't really exist. "My God," he
moaned, "but that's all we do. Our whole science is
based on breaking people up into categories so that we
can compare them to other groups."

I felt bad about that; after all, he's a good guy and
terribly concerned about finding ways for people to get
along with each other. But there's always more to people
than we can understand. People are real, but definitions
are always false, or at best useless, without a deeper
understanding.

I've listened to the earnest talk of people who are
struggling to understand a concept called "community"
and wondered what particular bit of earth, if any, they
hold dear. Like each individual, each community defies
definition, though not understanding.

Robert Frost understood. His poem "The Death of
the Hired Hand" probably comes as close as anything

I've read to the truth about community. In the poem, an old homeless drifter, sick and nearing death, returns to a farm where he'd worked for many years as a hired man. The farmer and his wife take him in, he grudgingly, she compassionately. In the course of a good-natured but earnest argument over the derelict's unexpected arrival and what they ought to do about it, they try to define the word "home."

"Home is the place where, when you have to go there, they have to take you in," he snorts.

"I should have called it something you don't have to deserve," she replies.

I find myself "returning" to this place that I have not left. Often, in some distant conversation about right and wrong, or love and hate, or the struggle to define what is or isn't, my thoughts come back to these few square miles of land and to the people who walk the same ground in their daily rounds as I do. It has become more important to me than I can say to know that we are all here, together.

HOME OF THE VIGILANTES

FOR JUSTICE

Nobody gets it and it's hard to explain, so I really got a kick out of Fair Share Bob's Myrtle Creek story.

My wife and I were in Veneta for the Oregon Country Fair, Lane County's annual summer counterculture extravaganza. The Emerald Empire, as Eugene and its environs are known, has a reputation for being Oregon's most liberal, politically correct community. But the Country Fair, even by Eugene standards, is a leftist event.

We were in Community Village, a little cul-de-sac of haphazard wooden booths housing dozens of radical activist organizations. The purest of the pure—goddess-worshiping New Age neo-pagans, Earth Firstlers, pro-hemp lobbyists, no-nukers, eco-feminists, and organic farmers—congregate there every summer, celebrate, and preach to the faithful. And here was Bob from Oregon Fair Share, an advocacy group for the poor, all excited about having done door-to-door canvassing in Myrtle Creek, my hometown.

"It was the weirdest thing," he began.

(Uh-huh.)

"I was a little worried about how they'd react to us anyway because it's supposed to be such a redneck area."

(Among the politically correct, Douglas County is known as one of the most hopelessly incorrect places in the state.)

"But the stats say it's really got some major economic problems . . ."

(At that time, a few years ago, they would have read something like: 14 percent unemployment, 17 percent poverty rate, 19 percent emergency food usage, 20 percent functional illiteracy.)

". . . and so we felt it was important to canvass down there and get the word out about Fair Share. You know, see what's really going on and all."

(Uh-huh.)

"So, we're coming into town and the first thing I see is that weird sign about the vigilantes."

WELCOME
Our streets
Patrolled by
MYRTLE CREEK'S
VIGILANTES for JUSTICE

"And I'm thinking, Oh my God! What are we getting into? So we go over to the city hall, because we have to register under the Green Valley Ordinance before we can go door to door, and they're all like, 'Well, okay, you can do it, but be careful—no telling what might happen.' So the first place we go to there's this pickup in the driveway with a gun rack and a bumpersticker that says 'Old F.A.R.T.—Fathers Against Radical Teenagers,' and now I'm really getting paranoid, you know?"

(Stephen King. Rod Serling. *Easy Rider. Deliverance.* Rednecks with shotguns and pickups—Oh my!)

"And this guy invites us in, and it turns out he's one of the Vigilantes, and we sit and have coffee and every-thing—talked to us for an hour. We couldn't get out of there, they just kept talking and giving us cookies and all. They were so nice. It turns out the Vigilantes are just a bunch of old guys with CBs, a Neighborhood Watch kind of thing."

"Everywhere we went it was like that. We'd planned to just spend a day in town, but it took us three days because everyone treated us so well. I couldn't believe it. Up here in Eugene they'll slam the door in your face sometimes but *nobody* was rude down there—they didn't give us any money, but everybody was just so friendly. Nicest bunch of people I ever met."

I laughed when he finished, but not out of derision for him or the town. I felt instead an overwhelming sense of pleasure, the kind of feeling you get when, after years of toying with a complex set of vague ideas and contradictory facts, all of your half-realized conclusions are suddenly confirmed. Just about everything you would ever learn about Myrtle Creek was contained in his little anecdote. I could have kissed him, but I couldn't stop laughing.

Everything they say about Myrtle Creek is true—sort of. They (our urban neighbors on the Willamette and Rogue) say it's a backwater place, the domain of ignorant, bible-thumping, "God, Guns, and Guts" hillbillies.

They (the folks who live here) say it's a friendly, progressive little town, combining the best of old-fashioned community values and modern development, a real nice place to raise your kids.

And they're both right—sort of. Besides, the truth is a little complicated and not nearly as believable, or as much fun, as the myths.

Take, for instance, the large wooden sign that greets you as you cross the bridge into town. The Chamber put it up, turning a weedy patch of hillside into a landscaped greeting scene.

Welcome to Myrtle Creek, Gateway to the One
Hundred Valleys of the Umpqua

it says, and hanging underneath they've added a white sign this year, "1893 Centennial 1993."

Setting aside the fact that no one has ever counted just how many valleys there are in the 5,000 mountainous square miles of Douglas County, it's hard to see Myrtle Creek as the gateway to much of anywhere. It's located a good thirty miles north of the Josephine County line and Interstate 5 bypasses the town on the other side of the river. You have to go out of your way to get into town, and the only two valleys that you actually have to pass through the city limits to get to are North Myrtle Creek and South Myrtle Creek.

Also, there's a controversial footnote to the centennial. Back in 1901 the state revoked Myrtle Creek's city charter for a couple of years due to the town's failure to collect enough taxes to operate. Some people argue that the two years without a charter makes it only ninety-eight years old, and others claim that the second charter was a new one and therefore the current town only goes back to 1903.

So, in all honesty, the sign should read something like: "Welcome to Myrtle Creek, Gateway to Two of the One Hundred (more or less, but nobody's really sure how many) Valleys of the Umpqua. 1893 (or 1903) Centennial (except maybe for two years when the town was bankrupt) 1993 (or 1995 or 2003 depending on who you ask)." As I said, the truth's not nearly as believable as the myths.

In Myrtle Creek boosterism reaches almost pathological proportions. The town hosts an incredible number of festivals, concerts, and amateur sports contests ranging from Babe Ruth Baseball state championships to wheelchair basketball fundraisers.

This flurry of public-spirited display has increased over the past decade or so as the town made painful adjustments to a series of economic disasters. The slump began with the Reagan recession of the early eighties, continued with the "lean and mean" (bosses got mean and workers got lean) Reagan "miracle" recovery, and, ever downward, slid into the Bush era of housing slumps and environmental litigation.

One early casualty was the annual Wood 'n' Nickel Days celebration, which had been held for more than twenty years. When the town's last mill shut down and Hanna Mining Company closed the Nickel Mountain strip mine and smelter in nearby Riddle, the celebration—in a town now lacking both lumber and nickel ore—was rechristened the Summer Arts Festival. Considering the times, maybe it should have been called the Unemployment Check and Government Surplus Cheese Festival, since that's what had become the mainstays of the local economy.

Desperate times call for desperate measures. After all, a town cannot live by food stamps alone. So when a local restaurateur suggested an annual race to help liven things up, the business community took up the challenge.

Most people don't know this, but, by crossing two pieces of lath and placing them on the back of a turkey and running fast enough to keep up, you can guide a panic-stricken bird more or less in a straight line. The hugely successful Turkey Grand Prix brought out happy crowds to watch local business leaders, dressed in appropriate costumes, sprint down Main Street behind live fowl.

It was great fun, but after a couple of years some animal-rights activists got upset and threatened to spoil the event with picket signs calling media attention to the "cruel and barbaric ritual." Despite the general consensus that anyone who feels sorry for a turkey must have never raised one, the Chamber caved in and switched to pushing frozen turkeys down the street in wheelbarrows and shopping carts. "PC" had come to Myrtle Creek at last, but it just wasn't the same, and the Turkey Grand Prix died out for lack of interest.

Millsite Park is another product of the hard times. In the late seventies work was started to convert an industrial wasteland, the former site of a mill that burned down in the fifties, into a city park.

The park, a volunteer project that is still underway, is a remarkable achievement for a town of 3,300 residents. So it's true that the old-fashioned barn-raising spirit of neighborliness is alive and well here. Which is not surprising because the people aren't too far removed—only a generation or so—from rural self-sufficiency.

City dwellers tend to forget that the word "neighbor" (from the German *Nachbar* by way of the Anglo-Saxon *neahgebur*, meaning "near farmer") is a rural word for a rural concept. "Civilization," on the other hand, comes from the Latin *civitas*, meaning "city." The two ideals are not really related. A place can be, and often is, neighborly without being terribly civilized, and the reverse also holds true. In fact, civility and neighborliness just might be notions as incompatible as urbanity and boorishness.

And that, in a nutshell, seems to be the source of the confusion about Myrtle Creek, both in its image outside the area and in its image of itself. Like other small rural towns all across the American West, Myrtle Creek is being carried headlong into the twenty-first century and making the painful transition from neighborliness to civility.

For two hundred years, country folk all over the world, under the relentless pressure of industrialization, have been forced from the self-sufficiency of the land into the wage dependency of the cities. Cut off, literally, from their roots, within a generation or two they lose their rural values, which were based on cooperation and broad common needs, and exchange them for the market ideal of narrow competitive goals. And there, as they say, goes the neighborhood.

~

The ancient bond of the *Nachbar* hood, already virtually extinct in American cities, lives on in Myrtle

Creek, at least for now. But here, too, it's starting to show wear and tear under the strains of civilization. The hard times of the eighties gave us both the renewed cooperative spirit that built a beautiful park and a new general atmosphere of betrayal, distrust, and fear.

Whenever there's private fear and desperation, there's always someone ready to focus it outward on a wider, less personal, unsolvable problem. After all, it's always easier to worry about something like "family values" than to think about what will happen to your own family if you can't make your next land payment. And once people get in the habit, it's easy to carry them along from one fear to the next.

Law and order, predictably, was the first one. The Vigilantes for Justice came out of the "get tough on crime" and "war on drugs" years. Next, yellow ribbon fever struck, and the town erupted with anti-environmentalist posters and, of course, yet another sign at the edge of town proclaiming Myrtle Creek a "Yellow Ribbon City" where "We Support the Timber Industry."

During the past five years, support has come to mean opposition. With a cornucopia of targets, a siege mentality has set in, and increasingly complex conspiracy theories go the rounds as the issues all become somehow intertwined. Sometimes it seems that everybody here is actively opposed to something. Actually though, what it amounts to is a sizable minority that is opposed to just about everything from Earth First! to the school board.

Despite the hard knocks of the past thirteen years and the changing nature of life in this valley, apathy, at least, is not much of a problem. Myrtle Creek is still a small enough town to provide its inhabitants with a sense of responsibility and the power to determine their own fate. This is a rare attitude nowadays, one that survives only in backwater places. It is like a rare flower pushed to the brink of extinction by the destruction of its natural habitat—which is a shame, because it is the essential ingredient for the type of democracy Thomas Jefferson saw as the great hope for America's future.

A DANGER TO THE COMMUNITY

ROADSIDE TRASH

The old guy wasn't as old as he'd looked, standing there all crumpled and discarded next to the interstate with his thumb out. Once he got in the truck I could read "wino" written in ravaged lines on his face, as plain as if it'd been printed with a black marker. He had furtive dumpster-picker eyes, half sly fox and half beaten dog. He also had a mild case of the shakes, either habitual tremors or from alcohol withdrawal. It's hard to tell unless you ask, which is a rude thing to do.

I regretted stopping to pick him up even before he sat down next to me, filling my pickup truck cab with his rummy smell. Picking up hitchhiking derelicts is a habit I can't seem to shake—probably a result of listening to too many nuns' stories about Jesus or Saint

Peter begging at the door in disguise. The poor bastards are harmless, though sometimes they're unpleasant company. Besides, I've never gotten the truly frightening, creepy feeling from a wino that I get regularly whenever I'm around glad-handing realtors or bankers or politicians.

"I ain't going far," I told him, "just down to Myrtle Creek."

"Well, every bit helps," he sighed. "I'm heading to Medford. How far is that? I'm not too far, am I?"

"No, it'll be about seventy miles from where I drop you off is all. With any luck you'll get there in an hour or so."

"Good," he said. "I'm in kind of a hurry. I want to get into a detox program. I heard there's one down there that might let me in. I tried here in Roseburg, but they said it'd take me six months 'cause I ain't got no money to pay for it."

That explained the shaking. I hoped he wouldn't start his delirium tremens before I dropped him off. A hard-core alky could die from sudden withdrawal without medical treatment.

"Yeah, well, that figures," I told him. "The place is packed with people who got busted on piss tests at work. They're too busy raking in the insurance money right now to mess with you." It was the spring of 1988, and random workplace urinalysis testing was a multimillion-dollar front in the latest election-year War on Drugs. "Take a look at this," he suggested and rolled up his shirtsleeve to reveal an impressive-looking crater in the crook of his arm.

"Did you show them that?" I wondered aloud.

"Yeah. Didn't do me no good though."

"Been waiting long?" I asked to change the subject.

"About four hours, I guess. Not bad, about average."

At four hundred cars per hour—the average traffic flow on that stretch of road—he'd watched 1,600 drivers pass him by.

"Yeah, that's not bad at all. I picked up a pair of Canadians there, a couple weeks back. They'd been stuck for fourteen hours."

"Jay-zus!"

"Yeah, they was bummed, couldn't believe it. They thought folks around here must be extra unfriendly or something. The fact is that people are just scared. A hitchhiker murdered a local gal here a couple years back, so nobody wants to give anybody a ride."

"Well, I can't say as I blame 'em. That's all it takes, one bad apple to screw it up for everybody else."

"Yeah, it's been in the papers for a long time, real brutal. Turned out the guy'd escaped from prison, and she picked him up on the freeway. The guy raped her, cut her throat, and stole her pickup. They caught him and there was a big trial and everything."

"Oh, Christ, that's sick. I mean, I can understand— a guy gets a little horny and what the hell, you know? But, shit-oh-dear, you don't gotta go and do something like that." He shook his head. "You know, we had a guy down in California years ago, raped a fifteen-year-old girl and chopped her arms off. Left her for dead."

"Lawrence Singleton."

"Yeah! That's right, Singleton, that was the guy's name. How'd you know that?"

"He's out on parole now. The papers are all full of it. Nobody wants him to live near them, and he can't find a place to live. He might be moving up here from California pretty soon."

"Here?"

"Yeah, he's got an invite from this preacher down in Azalea, about twenty miles south. The folks around here are pretty upset about it. There's going to be a meeting Saturday down at the Grange."

"God, I can see why. Who'd want a guy like that around?"

I dropped him off on the interstate on a spring morning six years ago, but, in a metaphorical sense, I guess I'm still hauling him around with me. I wonder sometimes whether he lived long enough to get the hospital bed and intravenous rehydration, the tranquilizers and food and vitamins that he obviously needed. I hope so. I hope that God really does have a special love for drunks and kids and crazy people, and that the old guy didn't just end up an anonymous corpse somewhere.

I think of him sometimes when I listen to the vague jargon of activists and politicians, people who speak in metaphors so much that it seems they never consider reality itself. The old guy "fell through the cracks in the system," though if he actually fell, he more than likely fell on some linoleum or concrete or asphalt, leaving an untidy "John Doe" cadaver for someone to haul off to the morgue, rather than dropping neatly down a metaphorical chasm in something as abstract as a system.

I never met Lawrence Singleton, alcoholic and parolee, but I've talked to many unwanted people. They're not hard to find in a country like ours, where lives are tossed away as casually as a cigarette butt.

GOD'S COUNTRY

My friend Esther called for some advice, or some help anyway. She'd been talking to one of the reporters who were asking everyone up and down the road questions about the Reverend Tom Smith and the Brides of Christ. It wasn't easy to explain why Smith and his flock were so unpopular with their neighbors or why that distrust had erupted into a national news story. Esther thought that I should talk to some of the television and newspaper reporters who were suddenly covering Azalea like maple bugs on a window screen.

"He was asking me about Smith's dog getting shot," she said, "and I tried to tell him about how it works around here if your dog gets into the neighbors' livestock, but he didn't understand. They're from back east, city people. How can you tell them it's okay to shoot a dog if it's killing your chickens?"

I imagined Esther trying to explain the complex etiquette of shooting your neighbor's dog to a journalist from back east. The reporter was probably accustomed to liquor store shootings, rapes, and muggings, but the notion of using a 30-06 on a trespassing mutt would strike him as petty barbarism rather than an unpleasant necessity sanctioned by law and custom.

Dogs, either on their own or in packs, will chase, maim, and often kill livestock. Sheep and poultry are particularly vulnerable, but calves and colts are sometimes mauled. A pair of dogs out on a lark can destroy thousands of dollars worth of sheep in a brief frenzy. Ranchers and farmers, faced with a marauding canine, shoot. If they miss, the county Animal Control officer will track down the offender and send it to the shelter for destruction, writing out a heavy fine for the dog's owner. The proper thing to do when your dog is shot by a neighbor is to apologize and pay for the damaged livestock and count yourself lucky to avoid the fine and court costs.

I could see how that might be tough to explain, at least in any form that would fit into a sound bite. I could also understand why the preacher and his flock might interpret the dog's untimely demise as harassment. After all, they really were an unpopular group, as the bullet holes in their bus and front porch proved.

When the Reverend Tom Smith bought half of Marmalade Farm from a friend of mine, he didn't mention that he'd be bringing his sixty-five-member flock to settle there. Nor did he say anything about other land purchases he was making: a home on Starveout Creek, another property downstream on Cow Creek, and a commercial building in Canyonville. The neighbors were more than a bit alarmed when a seemingly well-financed group of men, women, and children from Las Vegas appeared suddenly in their valley.

Azalea, Oregon, is not a town, just an old wood-frame general store with gas pumps and a post office, zip code 97410, serving about 250 homes. The people of Azalea live scattered along a twenty-five-mile stretch of Upper Cow Creek Road, which runs along a shoestring valley from I-5, where the store is located, into the mountains. It is one of hundreds of small valleys tucked between the tangled mountain ridges of southern Oregon, as isolated from each other as islands in the sea.

Although it has no city charter, the place comes as close as anywhere in America these days to being a community under the old-fashioned definition of a place where the residents know each other. Out in the boonies, what counts is not politics but neighborliness, the willingness to help each other simply because of proximity.

When the Brides of Christ showed up in Canyonville, people called them the "hankie-heads" because the group's women invariably wore bandannas tied over their hair, a style they had reportedly adopted due to some obscure biblical injunction. Seeing them at the Pioneer Super-Save or the Sears Mail-Order Store reminded me of the sharp-eyed old Russian women who used to live in North Dakota back in the fifties, though the *babushkas* favored long silk scarves tied under their chins rather than cotton kerchiefs tied at the nape of the neck. The look was a bit eccentric but appealing in a nostalgic sort of way.

They were a clannish bunch, not given to socializing much, which is bound to raise speculation. There was their "kiss of Christ" custom, for instance, some kind of an *agape* thing that they practiced, and with it the rumor that the women were brides of Reverend Smith as well as of Jesus. It was said that too many of the group's numerous children bore an uncanny resemblance to their spiritual and temporal leader. Was the kerchief a badge of servitude rather than modesty?

When a local paper revealed that Pastor Smith had a criminal record, which included a conviction for child molestation, folks took it as an affirmation of their suspicions and secret fantasies, proof that there was hanky-panky going on among the hankie-heads. Smith granted an interview in which he freely admitted his presalvation depravities and offered his sordid past as proof of God's great love for even the lowest of sinners. He also wondered if perhaps bigotry wasn't the real reason why he and his multiracial flock weren't getting along with the neighbors. Still, Jesus had warned that His followers would be persecuted, so it was to be expected.

An uneasy truce set in between the true believers and the community. The Brides were absolutely law-abiding and undeniably industrious. People began to assume a more tolerant attitude. After all, southern Oregon had a long history of eccentricity, ranging from nineteenth-century utopian experiments to the counter-cultural communes of the seventies.

The reverend began to mail out a monthly newsletter to local residents in an effort to promote understanding. Unfortunately, he succeeded. In a remarkable series of epistles, he laid out his convoluted teachings, drawing connections between apocalyptic biblical prophecy and a conspiracy theory linking Catholicism, Freemasonry, the Bavarian Illuminati, the Trilateral Commission, and the federal government (which is headquartered, it seems, in a city laid out in the form of a gigantic satanic talisman). Only a chosen few, Christ's brides, would survive the time of tribulations, which the Whore of Babylon was about to unleash from the power vector of evil located inside the Beltway.

Though the notion of a diabolical presence in the Reagan administration had a certain appeal, it was just too tidy and comforting. It would be heartening to find that there really is a purpose behind "the evil that men do," since that would be a sign of competence and intelligence.

Inviting Lawrence Singleton, former ax-wielding rapist, to live out his days in the bosom of the one true church was a very Christian thing to do. Certainly, even if nobody else wanted him, Jesus did, which is the nice thing about Jesus of Nazareth, equal-opportunity savior. The Lord never has been too particular about the company He keeps. Love them all—let God sort them out.

THE KLIEG
LIGHT CRUSADERS

The Reverend Smith didn't display much political savvy, but this deficiency was made up for at the Grange Hall meeting by an out-of-district U.S. congressman, two state assemblymen, and a half-dozen county officeholders—people who knew how to conduct themselves on a flag-draped podium and weren't uncomfortable in front of TV cameras.

The theme was crime and the speakers were vehemently, almost violently, opposed to it—certain forms of it, anyway. They didn't mention the crimes that had been committed against the Brides of Christ (who, while they'd outraged the community, hadn't broken any laws). But the crimes of Lawrence Singleton were condemned in suitably lurid terms. Although the possibility of personal forgiveness and redemption wasn't brought up, salvation for the entire community was offered through a crusade against crime.

The atmosphere was that of a revival tent. As the politicians denounced criminals and mollycoddling liberals equally, the audience grew palpably more right-eously enthusiastic. The expressions of uneasiness and concern on their faces gave way to a wolflike eager grin, showing confidence in the justness of their wrath.

By the time Congressman Denny Smith, the featured speaker, came to the podium to lay out his plans for mandatory sentencing, expeditiously applied capital punishment, and the building of camps "with Quonset huts and barbed wire and machine gun towers" over in eastern Oregon, I half expected him to lead an angry lynch mob in a march up to Marmalade Farm. Instead, he ended his speech, as had the others, with assurances that he would aid the community in ridding themselves of the cult that threatened them.

As it turned out, Congressman Smith went away after the klieg lights were shut off, and neither he nor the national press ever returned. Lawrence Singleton announced that he was moving to Florida rather than Oregon. The Brides of Christ packed up and left for eastern Washington a few years later. In the end, the only threat to the community turned out to be the secular cult of law and order and the demagogues who, for a few short weeks, exploited it.

DIRTY LAUNDRY

I was talking to Bob the Milkman in the laundromat in town. It's a spacious, comfortable, run-down old place of peeling paint and broken linoleum tiles, with worn-out machines that cough and spit and shake like epileptics. It was the kind of conversation that might have taken place in a coffeehouse or small café, where people gather to talk earnestly. But I'm not sure whether such places even exist anymore, and, even if they do, our little town doesn't have one.

"Well, I see the rate of entropy is increasing rapidly," he began, and he wasn't talking about the laundromat. We started out with the elections just a few days past and moved on quickly to politics, economics, apathy, alienation, television, and what passes these days for civilization—everything that has the stench of death or worse still, the sterile, inhuman lack of any smell at all.

....

We sat there, two aging hippies, engaged in the old eternal, foolish task of trying to find a meaning to it all, to make sense of the incomprehensible. Here among the dirty laundry, on a side street in a small town, we searched for a way to reverse entropy.

Bob was feeling even more cynical than usual. It was obvious to him that the world was rapidly heading for hell in a laundry cart. Of course, though he professed despair, he hadn't given up looking for solutions. It takes a lot of love to be a cynic; you have to care before you can be bitter.

"How?" he kept asking. "How can it be overcome? The technology is so pervasive. Television, for example, serves the status quo, and people have forgotten how to question the conditions that keep them powerless and apart—and one of the main ones is TV itself."

I'd been stewing in the juices of my own personal despair when he came in with his broken wicker baskets filled with clothes, so it did my heart good to leave my clothes in the dryer after they were done and take up the defense of the good old cause for a while. It's amazing how the cleansing action of social optimism can scrub the embarrassing stains from your soul.

We talked of the impending war, of the savings and loan scandal, of the power of advertising to subvert reason, and of the loss of hope in the daily struggle to pursue happiness through the endless swamp of major and minor restrictions to liberty.

....

It was a sort of game, like playing checkers with social principles, his black negative pieces to my red positives. Sitting on a pair of wooden benches, scarred with the jackknife-engraved history of our town's romances, we faced each other over the board of life, finding friendly pleasure in something we both took quite seriously.

He opened with the deception and hypocrisy of politics.

I countered with the wisdom of common people.

He didn't doubt the wisdom but what about apathy, the sense of powerlessness?

"Lack of power breeds frustration, a powerful emotion that brings change," I maintained.

"Only if it's a shared frustration, otherwise it just increases separation and distrust, leaving us ripe for manipulation by demagogues."

"People know, deep down, that they need each other. Eventually people realize that things like dignity and justice and freedom are real needs—things we can't live without. If they're denied us, we'll get together and demand them."

That one shook him some; I could see it in his expression as he searched for a response.

"But who are we anyway? Where is our sense of common purpose, of ourselves as a people? People have to have something in common in order to band together. We've been reduced to seeing ourselves as individuals, cut off from each other, mere consumers with conflicting self-interests. There has to be some common ground."

"Well, there's always the sense of place, the realization that the common ground is right here beneath our feet. We are, in fact, neighbors here."

"That's an antique notion. People don't live in a place anymore."

"Whether they realize it or not, they do. It can't be denied because it's a physical fact. We share this valley. That's reality, and reality is awfully stubborn—it keeps coming up no matter how much we ignore it."

"It comes up, but what if we don't have the ability to see it anymore? Our language has become debased by the system. It's so damn pervasive. We can't even think clearly anymore because words have become meaningless from being twisted to serve the status quo. All we have left is a vague, generalized discontent and no tools to examine it with. Whatever happened to the search for meaning? It's died out. People used to talk about this stuff all the time. It was important to them. What happened to all that?"

Well, he had me there. I thought of the world I came of age in, the late sixties and early seventies, and how tough it is to explain those times to teenagers. The kids see the shell of those days—long hair and tie-dyes, rock 'n' roll and LSD—but it's incredibly hard to tell them about our idealism, our search for basic human values, and our commitment to passé notions like truth and justice and peace and love. I was struck by how odd we two were, as anachronistic as two old white-bearded Jews discussing one of the fine points of Kabbalah.

"Yes, it's pretty much gone now," I admitted, "but not entirely. There's always going to be the misfits, the oddballs like us, who sense something's wrong and go looking for the answers. It will always crop up in little pockets here and there and—who knows?—maybe some of those seeds will take off and grow."

"Yes, a few seeds will grow, but they'll be stunted. The ground's gone barren. The soil's been sterilized. Hell, people don't even read books anymore."

"Yeah, most of my friends don't read books at all, and the ones that do, read garbage. The only people I know who actually read literature are all writers. It's discouraging. It haunts me. I don't know, maybe we need to find ways around that—storytelling or something. Maybe if we can find the right kind of manure, the seeds will have a chance."

"Maybe, but don't count on it."

There wasn't much more we could say. He'd shaken my optimism and I'd rattled his pessimism, and, strange as it may seem, we were both happier for it.

Outside, one of our town's shattered, shell-shocked military veterans wandered by under gray November skies, wrapped in his personal cloud, searching for cigarette butts, lost in a forgotten war. Who knows? Maybe Bob's right. Maybe we're all becoming shell-shocked, on the road to becoming lost souls, searching for a happiness fix on the sidewalks of life.

I gathered up the warm clean clothes, loaded them in my battered pickup, and drove the autumn roads home, searching for the right kind of manure.

FALLING ASHES

The sunset shadow of the mountain creeps across the bottomlands toward the river. It's a late October afternoon in the valley, almost Halloween, and along the river the trees of autumn are bright in the sun. The strip of trees along the river forms a leaf-mosaic of gold, green, yellow, and brown, and even from a distance each leaf is distinct, outlined in shadow. The salmon-road river quietly flows through the bottoms, low but on the rise, cleaning out the summer algae, waiting for the seasonal creeks to appear.

Across the river a peach orchard in red and yellow lies surrounded by flat fields, squares of green sheep-dotted pasture, hay fields, and wheat stubble. Orange pumpkins lie in their bed of frost-bitten vines, ready for the knives that will give them baleful eyes and jack-o'-lantern grins. The setting sun shows the snake-braid course of the old river channels, still visible a century after the soil-building marsh was drained.

The distant black figures of humpbacked men move along the edge of a brown field. Their outstretched arms taper into bronze rods that drip molten lava. A line of flames marches across the stubble, crackling hungry flame-tongues lapping up the harvest chaff, making the soil ready for another crop of winter wheat. The smoke of autumn rises, making a reddish golden glow in the setting sun's light. The hills and mountains are distant-seeming, dark and haze-hidden.

Behind the smoke, Interstate 5 crosses the bottom-land, as final and unswerving as an exercise in geometry. Beneath the crackling sound of the fire the highway adds the softened thrum of diesel engines and a rubbery shush of eighteen-wheeled semitrucks. Like ants bearing the harvest, they follow each other in a busy endless line stretching north and south.

Close at hand, leaves pirouette in their brief moments of freedom and land with a soft crackling. Jays call raucously, quail and finches rustle in the poison oak brush in search of seeds. A wide-eyed calf gallops across the pasture to the safety of his mother's side. The old dog stares out across the valley, nose pointed toward the smoke, whining nervously as she smells the scent of the death of an Indian summer afternoon.

ROTOTILLING RESURRECTION

"Spring has now unwrapped the flowers, day is fast
   arriving

Life in all her growing powers toward the light is
   striving

Gone the iron touch of cold, winter time and frost
   time

Seedlings working through the mould now make
   up for lost time.

"Herbs and plants that winter-long slumbered at
   their leisure

Now bestirring green and strong, finding growth
   and pleasure

All the world with beauty fills, gold and green
   enhancing

Flowers make glee among the hills and set the
   meadows dancing."

⌒ "The Carol of the Flowers"
Sixteenth century, traditional

....

Waltzing my tiller, I wore a blister in the palm of my hand. I've gotten soft, apparently, sitting around all winter with the rain and snow outside my window, long days spent shifting a flickering cursor from line to line on my computer's cathode-ray tube. It's hard to accept soft hands that, even with canvas gloves on, blister from work.

I used to take pride in my scarred and calloused hands and swore that they'd never be soft. But it's been years since I bucked hay or peeled poles or set chokers. A little firewood cutting to keep us warm, some yard work once in a while, and perhaps a bit of shingling or carpentry once or twice a year is about the extent of my laboring now.

The scars remain but the protective calluses are gone. My hands are as soft as a butcher's or, worse yet, as soft as an editor's. I swore that I'd never lose touch with the gritty, hard, and lumpy world of physical reality. I would stand, ankle deep, my rubber boots in manure, shovel in hand, and tell myself how much easier the real stuff is to deal with than the metaphorical kind. And yet, I've gone soft now, become a presser of buttons and a peddler of metaphors. I fight it, but it's difficult not to become what you despise.

Rototilling helps. Everyone ought to go to bed tired and wake up hungry, of course, but exercise done for its own sake has always struck me as a sign of decadence. The sight of an exercise machine in the corner makes me shudder with visions of caged hamsters running on squeaky

....

wheels. Besides, it's hard for me to understand why any-one would work up a sweat and not get paid for it.

It may seem odd, but spending a few hours operating a roaring, clattering machine that's constantly bouncing and vibrating beneath my hands and raising clouds of dust is soothing work. Although it requires an acute level of physical attention (otherwise you could easily amputate a foot), it's not mentally demanding at all.

Spring weather is playful, and being out there in the shifting sunlight under a blue and white tie-dyed sky, feet sinking into the earth and head in the clouds, is a wonderfully expansive feeling after a winter spent cloistered indoors. The earth reveals its hidden secrets, the colors and smells of the varying soils. Quartz, agate, and jasper, bones, old bricks, colored glass and pottery shards and silverware, lost marbles, and toy soldiers all come popping up, revealed by the whirling tines.

Every spring I take out an ad in our local weekly paper and hire myself out as a tillerman. My customers are mostly old folks who have a small garden patch to prepare and not enough energy to dig it up by hand anymore. For some, the backyard garden is an essential source of food they wouldn't be able to afford otherwise. For others, it's just something to help relieve the tedium of television and medication and visits to the doctor.

Rich or poor (and mostly they're very poor), they all need their little bit of freshly turned soil. It's hard for them, in a world that no longer needs their labor, to find a way to apply their useful skills. Talking with them about the weather and mulch and compost over coffee and cookies during my vernal visits, I get the impression that battling weeds is really their way of battling inertia and death.

In my first few tilling seasons, I naively imagined that it would be good to work for free. Of course, I couldn't (and still can't) afford to do that. And yet, it seemed a noble notion, to do a good turn for these impoverished old people, perhaps to pay back a little of the respect that life had cheated them of in their "golden years."

When we talk about soils and fertilizers and varieties of vegetables, age is not part of it. I am simply the hired man, and we talk about the work at hand. There is no condescension or pity involved. Our roles are clear, employer and employee, and we respect each other on the basis of our knowledge and labor and skills.

Of course, they need me to prepare their ground. But lately I've begun to understand that they need me, as much or perhaps more, to sit and listen to them as gardeners, and that my wage, which they can't afford to pay and which I can't afford to decline, is the only way we can honestly honor each other. It is the precisely calculated measure of our respect, for ourselves and for each other.

BLACK WINGS

Visitors to the Umpqua Valleys are always a little disappointed when they find out that the big soaring birds they've been admiring aren't eagles after all but turkey vultures—what we call buzzards here.

"Oh . . .," they say. "Buzzards, huh?" and then they change the subject, embarrassed at having mistaken a common carrion eater for the Lord of the Skies.

You can't blame them really. It has to be a letdown when the bold, sharp-eyed hunter you thought you saw turns out to be someone who dines on road-kill possum. They suspect that somehow they've been taken in by a shabby impostor, and even if you don't laugh outright, they know they've made the kind of mistake that country people enjoy seeing their city friends blunder into.

Of course, we never tell them how right their first instincts were, that we often pause to watch the birds ourselves, because their spiral soaring fills us with delight.

....

It's a local secret, something we don't often mention to each other—let alone admit to outsiders—but buzzards are beautiful.

Springtime comes to the valleys on black wings when the first buzzards return from their winter vacations in the deserts of Arizona and California. They come in from on high, tiny specks riding the wind, dropping lower and lower to sail along the rock faces and cliffs, wobbling like kites as they spread out over the valleys.

On sunny mornings after a rainy night they sit in snags and spread their wings, drying their feathers. They're sociable birds, patrolling with their friends and relatives or just roosting together, five or six to a tree. They don't seem to mind sharing a meal. There's plenty to go around, and besides, in their line of work I'd imagine one can't be too proud or fussy.

Though the buzzards migrate, they spend the better part of the year, nine months, right here, breeding and nesting and raising their young just like we do. Like good country folk everywhere, they don't ask for much, just a chance to live quietly and peaceably among their friends and neighbors, getting by on what the land has to offer.

In late fall, when the cold comes and the valleys cool, no longer sending up thermal drafts for the buzzards to ride, they gather together, fifty or sixty in a flock, waiting for the right wind to take them south. One morning you wake up and they're gone, and the skies are suddenly emptier and more lonely.

....

OLD-TIMERS

Years ago, I lived in Los Angeles without a car or money for bus rides. I hitch-hiked daily and spent hours beside the rivers of cars, fishing for a ride. As I peered at the faces behind the windshields, I became fascinated by the expressions of the drivers. At first, I was struck by the great variety of people and later by the habitual masks they wore when no one was there to watch.

Faces tell us many things about people. The history of our lives is etched in lines of hope and fear, joy and sadness, caring and indifference for all to plainly see. Our passing emotions leave permanent traces at the corners of our eyes and mouths, and as we grow older the sum of our inner life becomes more and more evident to everyone we meet.

Younger people can seem neutral in their look, pre-occupied or bored perhaps, but with almost no visible hint of their outlook in their aspect. Old people, though, seem either happy or sad when alone and not thinking of anything in particular. It's as if life itself, that master gardener, had patiently shaped them like potted bonsai. I remember pointing this out to my wife one afternoon as we stood at a traffic light on Eagle Rock Boulevard, in northeast Los Angeles. We were very young then, she sixteen and I eighteen, and we made a pact to be happy-faced in our old age.

Half a lifetime after those sidewalk days in Los Angeles I'm still watching faces, and as my appreciation has grown for just how difficult life really is, my fascination with the beauty of elderly men and women has grown too.

My younger brother calls them grimsters, short for "grim-faced old men with caps," and you see a lot of them around here, driving by in their weathered pickup trucks, dressed in hickory shirts, feed caps, and overalls or Lee 88's with suspenders. Their faces are as worn as old work gloves. They're retired loggers, farmers, miners, and Mill workers mostly, and most people just call them old-timers.

Visitors from the crowded warrens of asphalt and fluorescent lighting where most Americans live often mistake the look for unfriendliness or bitterness. They remember television shows and movies featuring unsuspecting tourists caught in sinister small towns where violence lurks behind the hard sidelong glances of lounging rednecks, and they grow uneasy.

People fear what they don't understand, of course. To me, bankers and accountants are scary people, and the thought of a Chamber of Commerce luncheon fills me with a nameless horror and dread.

The old men my brother classified by their grim expressions are almost always kind, gentle, and full of humor and mischief when you listen to them talk. Though they have their share of regrets, I never get a sense of bitterness or frustration from them. Their faces record a life of orneriness, determination, patience, and resignation.

I spent two summers working for McCormick Piling Company in Riddle, Oregon, hand-peeling bark from logs destined to become power-line poles. It was the last pole yard in the state where machinery hadn't taken over the job, and it closed down four or five years later during the Reagan "trickle-down" recession.

Pole peelers are now as extinct as the grizzly bears who used to live in these mountain valleys. Maybe it's all for the best. I'm not sure I really need half-ton predators who run the 100-meter dash in the low sixes ambling around my pasture, and I can't honestly say that I wish I was still chipping bark from sixty-foot logs at eight cents per linear foot for a living. But still, something is missing here, gone forever, and the valley somehow isn't the same.

It was fairly hard work, and if you didn't have the right attitude and technique it could be brutal. Only old men could last long at it. High school kids, attracted by the notion of doing piecework with no time clock to punch, would show up and beg for a load of logs to peel. None of them ever lasted long, most would knock out half a load and give up. But the four regular peelers, men in their sixties and seventies, kept at it day after day, wielding their double-bit axes, spud bars, and peavy poles at a steady, unhurried pace that the impatient young athletes couldn't match.

I was used to keeping up. Laboring is very competitive, and I took pride in being able to work right alongside, and sometimes outwork, men my age and younger who were four inches taller and forty pounds heavier than me. After six years on construction sites and in the woods, I considered myself as physically and mentally tough as anyone I'd ever worked with. But every time I paused to straighten my back and wipe the sweat off my eyelids, I'd look over at the old-timers and they'd be ahead of me.

The hardest lessons to learn are the ones you think you already know. I'd always used my head and my heart to beat men whose size and strength I couldn't match. Big guys rely on strength, little guys use technique, pacing, and endurance.

I was always looking for ways to make my work quicker and easier, handling heavy materials with good body mechanics, laying out my work efficiently, pacing myself for the long run, and simply resolving to endure whatever pain and fatigue the workweek demanded. It took me a month to understand that I was being beaten at my own game by grizzled masters who could work a young buck like me to death.

As the weeks wore on, I came to know them. We'd help each other free poles that were unusually large or jammed in the deck. Slowly, in laconic bits and pieces of advice, they taught me the tricks of their anachronistic craft. "Let me see yer spud bar. Not bad, gotta good weight and the curve's about right, but see here? Your edge's sharpened up on ya. Gotta dull it some or it'll bite through the bark instead of slipping under." A bastard file would appear from a back pocket, three smooth swipes across the edge and it would come back to me. "Here, try 'er now. That spring steel gets sharper when you use it."

As the summer wore on, our conversations got longer and further removed from the task at hand. They knew a lot, those old men, and I found out how to do many things that modern technology had made obsolete: how to sharpen the old two-man "misery whip" saws, how to load piling on railroad flatcars with mules, how to hand-hew a tree trunk to make an octagonal sailing ship's mast ninety feet tall.

Not so long ago, most Americans lived in the countryside, and even those who lived in cities made their

living as blue-collar workers. My grandfather, Lawrence
Heilman, still farmed with Belgian draft horses in the
forties and early fifties as he had done on his father's farm
in czarist Russia before the turn of the century. People
tend to think of those times, with a mixture of romantic
sentimentalism and condescension, as simpler times.

Nothing could be less accurate than to say those
times were simple. Getting by in the old days, from
"Whan Adam dalfe and Eve span" to 1950, required
intimate, complex, and sophisticated knowledge. My
grandfather was illiterate but he could read a team of
eight draft horses as easily as I scan newspaper headlines.

What we yearn for in the past is not simplicity but
the certainty and self-assurance of those times, something that has died out in our culture within a single
generation. Our lives here in the Information Age have
become as temporary and transitory as the flickering
cursor on a computer monitor. We have lost the sure
knowledge of our bodies, the physical education that
literally kept us in daily touch with the world around us.
Henry Miller, back in the 1940s, wrote of *The Air-
Conditioned Nightmare*, which the American Dream was
becoming. Today, that nightmare has become our daily
reality and we dream of "simpler" times.

The old-timers know that their world has passed.
They know full well that it was a brutal and ignorant time
in many ways. One and all they believe in the inevitabil-
ity of progress and think it good. The hope of a better life

and the pride in helping it come about sustained them through hard and bitter times, through deaths of friends in war and at work, through the despair of economic slumps, labor strikes, and false promises, through a life of pain and labor. They have arrived at last, tough and gnarled as ancient oaks, in the promised land only to find themselves in a world that doesn't seem to need them, where the old virtues of endurance, self-reliance, orneriness, and integrity don't count for much.

"You know," one of my fellow pole peelers confessed one day, "I don't need the money I make here. I've got a pension and Social Security and all that. My land's all paid for and I could take it easy, but I've worked so damn hard for so long, it's the only thing I know. If I stopped working I'd just up and die."

A few years ago two elderly women from Siskiyou County, about 120 miles south of the Umpqua in northern California, were driving from Yreka to Crescent City on a two-lane mountain road when their car went over the bank and down a steep hillside through the brush. Both of them were injured in the crash, and because of the rugged remoteness of the place, they spent two days helping each other crawl back up the slope to the road, where they flagged down a passing trucker who took them to a hospital. When a news reporter asked them how they managed to survive the ordeal, one of them replied simply, "We are women and we are strong."

I laughed when I read that because I have a neighbor who undoubtedly would have done and said the same thing if it had happened to her.

Alice is in her late eighties or maybe early nineties now, and she lives alone in a rocky canyon about a quarter of a mile up the road from me. I'm her nearest neighbor, and over the years I've watched her place for her during her solitary trips throughout the western United States, when she drives the mountain and desert roads, collecting rare wildflowers to plant in her rock garden.

Years ago she asked me to keep an eye on her place for a few months. At eighty-two she was having her knees replaced with artificial joints because her arthritis was keeping her from gardening. For three months I stopped by every day and fed the dog and cat and kept an eye out for vandals, until one day I spotted her pickup truck sitting in the driveway.

I walked up to the house and saw her crutches lying by the toolshed, but she was nowhere around. I called her name and walked around looking for her, worried that something might have happened. Visions of her lying on the ground helpless filled me with increasing fear as I searched, circling outward from the house.

Finally, I heard her calling my name from up the canyon, so I set off up the steep trail along the creek. I found her carefully picking her way down the path, leaning on a shovel in one hand and a pick in the other, her knees still wrapped in bandages from the operation.

"Been up cleaning out my spring box," she explained. "Got to get the water working again so I'll be ready for planting. My garden club's coming out next month for a tour. You know any teenagers I can hire that ain't too lazy to put in a good day's work?"

Professional storyteller and writer Robert Leo Heilman began to write after a roofing accident prevented him from continuing seasonal labor. His essays, articles, and interviews have appeared in many literary journals and anthologies, and in regional commentary on National Public Radio. An avid baseball card collector, he lives with his wife and son in Myrtle Creek, Oregon. Heilman was awarded the Northwest Writers 1996 Andres Berger Award for *Overstory: Zero*.